Every Day with Jesus

MAY/JUN 2019

God's New Society

'on this rock I will build my church' Matthew 16:18

Selwyn Hughes
Revised and updated by Mick Brooks

© CWR 2019. Dated text previously published as *A Fresh Look at the Church* (May/June 2006) by CWR. This edition revised and updated for 2019 by Mick Brooks.

CWR, Waverley Abbey House, Waverley Lane, Farnham, Surrey GU9 8EP, UK **Tel: 01252 784700**
Email: mail@cwr.org.uk Registered Charity No. 294387. Registered Limited Company No. 1990308.

Cover image: Stocksy/Dejan Ristovski
Quiet Time image: Pixabay/DesignNPrint
Printed in England by Linney

MIX
Paper from
responsible sources
FSC® C015900
www.fsc.org

CWR

A word of introduction...

The streets would have been noisy, bustling, packed with pilgrims from all over the country for the mandatory holiday. It's at this moment in time that the Holy Spirit swept into the life of the Church. The Holy Spirit suddenly and unexpectedly facilitated a hectic coming-together of lifestyles, cultures and religion into a new society. Imagine witnessing such a disparate gathering of diverse people, races, classes and theological persuasions forming the foundations of one of the most radical and remarkable movements in history. Even more amazing is the fact that in spite of dispersion and intense persecution, the Church has not only survived, but its influence and lasting impact remains embedded in practically every nation in the world.

To have been part of the Early Church would have been exhilarating, exciting, disconcerting and at times deeply uncomfortable. This issue explores how the Early Church grappled with many of the issues that the Church of today still continues to wrestle with: issues of money, leadership, ethics, and clashes with ruling authorities.

One of Selwyn's passions was that the Church would rediscover its roots, learn from past mistakes, and build upon those first foundations of living every day with Jesus – that each and every one of us would discover the part that we were born to play in service of 'God's New Society'.

Mick

Mick Brooks, Consulting Editor

Back to the future

FOR READING & MEDITATION – EPHESIANS 3:1–13

'His intent was that now, through the church, the manifold wisdom of God should be made known' (v10)

Today we begin a series of meditations on the nature and characteristics of the Christian Church – what John Stott called 'God's New Society'. One of the best ways to discover how Church life was established and lived out is to look at the Acts of the Apostles, and that is where we will be spending much of our time. But on this opening day I must give you a warning: be ready to be challenged. For many, church life today is so very different to the Church's beginning on the Day of Pentecost. One theologian who studied in depth the differences between the Church of the first century and that of today said: 'The more I study the Early Church, the more I am convinced that we are desperately in need of a return to first principles and the ethos of the Acts of the Apostles.'

This theologian was not the only one to have made that observation. In the late 1940s, when Billy Graham was working as a Youth for Christ evangelist, he hosted an outreach event in Los Angeles. Thousands came to Christ, including many Hollywood celebrities. When the crusade was over, a group of ministers wrote to a newspaper complaining, 'Billy Graham has set the Church in Los Angeles back a hundred years.' When Billy heard this he is reported to have commented, 'Oh dear, I am so sorry… I was really trying to set it back 2,000 years!'

It is my conviction that every local church would do well to study the Acts of the Apostles with a view to identifying first principles. One thing is certain: if the Church of the twenty-first century reflects the principles and purposes of the Church of the first century, then there is considerable hope for the future.

FURTHER STUDY

Psa. 85:6;
Hab. 3:1–19

1. What was Habakkuk's prayer?

2. What was his attitude?

My Father and my God, open our eyes that we may see – really see – how we, Your people, can truly walk in Your plans and Your purposes. Begin with me, I pray. In Jesus' name. Amen.

'The Great Contemporary'

FOR READING & MEDITATION – ACTS 1:1–5

'In my former book, Theophilus, I wrote about all that Jesus began to do and to teach' (v1)

There is little doubt that the author of Acts is Luke, who travelled with Paul (Col. 4:14) and dedicated both his Gospel and Acts to a man named Theophilus. In the first five verses of the opening chapter of Acts, Luke sums up what he had dealt with in the 24 chapters of his Gospel – the purpose of Christ's coming to this world, His suffering on the cross, His resurrection, His appearance and instructions to the apostles, His promise of the Holy Spirit, and His ascension to heaven.

One word in the opening sentence tells us what the book is all about: 'began'. What Jesus began in the Gospels is continued in Acts. The Saviour had not finished when He ascended on high and returned to the royal throne. Through the Holy Spirit, He continues ministering in the lives of those committed to Him. Luke's opening statement could be paraphrased in this way: 'In this second book I am dealing with the things Jesus continues to do even though He is not around to be seen. He died, rose again from the dead, ascended to the Father – but now He is back. And how!'

FURTHER STUDY

Phil. 1:1–7;
Heb. 12:2

1. What was Paul's confidence?

2. Why should we fix our eyes on Jesus?

Make no mistake about it: it is the risen Christ we see at work in the Acts of the Apostles, moving in the hearts of men and women and bringing them into His Church. The ministry of Jesus may have had a beginning, but it will never have an ending. Someone has written of Jesus, 'You can never catch up with Him as He is always going before – the Great Contemporary.' This ever present and ever active ministry of Jesus through the Holy Spirit means we will never have a complete biography of our Lord Jesus Christ. How can there be of someone who forever lives?

Lord Jesus, I am so thankful that the ministry You began when You came to this earth continues still, and I long that people today should become as aware of You as were the men and women of that first century. Help us, dear Saviour. Amen.

Why a Church at all?

FOR READING & MEDITATION – MATTHEW 16:13–20

'on this rock I will build my church, and the gates of Hades will not overcome it.' (v18)

Before we start to go through the Acts of the Apostles, we pause to ask ourselves these important questions: what is the Church, and why does it exist?

Many people associate the Church with tall Gothic buildings, stained-glass windows and robed clergy. However, a church building is just a structure in which the Church worships. The Church is comprised of a farmer ploughing in a field, somebody at the kitchen sink, a student in a classroom, a mechanic in a garage, a business person at their desk, and so on. Wherever there is a heart that is redeemed and beats in unison with the heart of Christ – there a part of the Church exists. The Church is people – people who share the love of Jesus.

But why is there a Church at all? We remember that Jesus commissioned it. Deliberately He said, 'On this rock I will build my church.' The Church was not the idea or invention of the disciples. After Christ's death they did not decide, 'Let's get together and form a movement called the Church.' It was founded by Jesus and is a divine institution and revelation. There are many reasons why the Church was established, including to be His Bride (Rev. 21:2). But one of the main reasons for the Church being on earth is, as we saw earlier, to continue the work which He began. This is the exciting thing about the book of Acts – it shows us that what Christ once did, the Church was now doing. In terms of increase and the number of miracles that were performed, greater things happened through Christ in His Church than through Christ in the flesh. Let's not forget it was Christ in His Church that turned the ancient world upside down (Acts 17:6, AV)!

FURTHER STUDY

Matt. 18:15–20;
Eph. 5:22–33

1. What did Jesus declare about the assembly of His Church?

2. What relationship did Paul liken the Church to?

Father, forgive us that by our lack of faith and courage we, Your present-day Church, tie Your hands and limit Your power. You long for Your Church to be bold and adventurous. Revive us again and set our hearts on fire for You. Amen.

'They're drunk!'

FOR READING & MEDITATION – ACTS 2:1–13

'Some... made fun of them and said, "They have had too much wine."'
(v13)

It is impossible for me to give you a verse-by-verse exposition of the Acts of the Apostles – this would have to be spread over several issues of *Every Day with Jesus*. So what I would like to do is to focus on some of the distinctives that made the Early Church the influence it was. Then we shall compare the Early Church with the Church of the present day to explore the differences and any adjustments we may need to make.

The first of these distinctives is this: the empowering ministry of the Holy Spirit. Without doubt, the day on which the Holy Spirit came upon the waiting disciples – the Day of Pentecost – is one of the greatest days in the history of the Church. When the Holy Spirit fell, His coming produced a transformation in the lives of ordinary everyday people, who became extraordinary people doing extraordinary things in extraordinary ways. A little while after they had received the Holy Spirit, they stepped out into the street, speaking in languages they had never learned. This strange phenomenon, and perhaps also the flushed look on their faces, caused some to yell, 'They're all drunk!'

FURTHER STUDY

Isa. 29:13;
Col. 2:20;
2 Tim. 3:1–5

1. What did Paul have to write to the Colossians?

2. What did Paul warn Timothy of?

The two main accusations directed at the early Christians – 'They're drunk' and 'They're mad' – are rarely heard today. Most twenty-first-century Christians do not come under such suspicion, though that is hardly to our credit. What would happen if we opened ourselves up to the Spirit as eagerly and responsively as did the Early Church? People would say the same about us as they said about the first believers: they're drunk and they're mad. Maybe the fact that they don't ought to be a matter of the greatest concern.

Father God, forgive us when we lack the empowering of your Spirit in our Christian walk. Revive and refresh us today and help us to show You to others by our conduct and our character. In Jesus' name. Amen.

CWR Ministry Events

PLEASE PRAY FOR THE TEAM

DATE	EVENT	PLACE	PRESENTER(S)
1 May	Inspiring Women Day: Second-Hand Smoke	Waverley Abbey House	Diane Regan
9 May	Discipleship Toolbox	WAH	Andy Peck
11 May	Waverley Abbey College Open Day	WAH	WAC team
15 May	Great Chapters of the Bible: The Eternal Time Lord	WAH	Philip Greenslade
16 May	The Leadership Road Less Travelled	WAH	Andy Peck
23 May	Navigating Finances: God's Will and Your Money	WAH	Andy Peck
5 Jun	Preaching: From Bible Text to Engaging Sermon	WAH	Andy Peck
5 Jun	Summer Studies: Gifts of the Spirit	WAH	Andy Peck
10–14 Jun	Introduction to Biblical Care and Counselling	WAH	Louise Dyer, Rob Jackson and team
14–16 Jun	Bible Discovery Weekend	WAH	Philip Greenslade
19 Jun	The Bible in a Day	WAH	Andy Peck
21–23 Jun	Inspiring Women Summer Weekend: Crowned with Honour	WAH	Elizabeth Hodkinson and the Inspiring Women team
28 Jun	Healthy You: Healthy Schools: A Focus on You, the Leader	WAH	Derek Holbird

Please pray for our students and tutors on our ongoing courses in Counselling and Spiritual Formation at Waverley Abbey College (taking place at Waverley Abbey House).

We would also appreciate prayer for our ongoing ministry in Singapore and Cambodia, as well as the many regional events that will be happening around the UK this year.

For further information and a full list of CWR's courses, seminars and events, call **(+44) 01252 784719** or visit **cwr.org.uk/courses**

You can also download our free Prayer Track, which includes daily prayers, from **cwr.org.uk/prayertrack**

The true euphoria

FOR READING & MEDITATION – ACTS 2:14–21

'These men are not drunk, as you suppose.' (v15)

Yesterday we ended with the thought that if we lived nearer to the heart of our faith, and were in closer touch with the Holy Spirit, we too might need to answer the suspicion that we are either drunk or unhinged. Alcohol provides temporary relief from day to day. It picks you up but then lets you down. Not to mention the various long-term harmful effects. The Holy Spirit instils a true joy. He picks you up without letting you down.

Permit me to ask you two personal questions: does your contact with the Holy Spirit energise you? Does He produce in you feelings of contentment and joyfulness? Has anyone ever decided that because of your commitment to Jesus you are somewhat unhinged or drunk? Don't let anyone tell you that devotion and exuberance cannot go together. They can.

FURTHER STUDY

Matt. 3:1–11;
Luke 11:13;
24:49

1. What did John the Baptist prophesy?

2. What did Jesus promise?

Peter stood up on the Day of Pentecost to explain to the crowd that what they were witnessing was not a euphoria produced by alcohol; rather, he and the others were all under the influence of God's Holy Spirit. As he proceeds to unpack the truth about Jesus – His death, resurrection and ascension, and the outpoured Spirit – people suddenly cry out, 'What shall we do?' (v37). Within a short time 3,000 souls are added to the Church.

One talk, anointed by the Spirit, is responsible for bringing 3,000 people to the foot of the cross. 'Nowadays,' as someone has wryly remarked, 'in some places we might have to preach 3,000 sermons to bring one person to the foot of the cross.' Why the difference – especially since we in the twenty-first century have the same Holy Spirit? Perhaps this is the answer: it's one thing to have the Holy Spirit; it's another thing for the Holy Spirit to have us!

Lord God, drive out every fear that hinders my willingness to be fully empowered by You. Whet my appetite for You and Your Spirit. I long to be alive to You, intoxicated by You, filled with Your Spirit. In Jesus' name. Amen.

3,000 resurrections!

FOR READING & MEDITATION – ACTS 2:22–41

*'When the people heard this, they were cut to the heart and said...
"Brothers, what shall we do?"' (v37)*

Today we continue thinking about the impact of the Spirit on the Church during the Day of Pentecost – page one of Church history! One interesting thing about the book of Acts – the only reliable account of the beginning of the Christian Church – is that on almost every page the Holy Spirit can be seen at work. It has often been said that if you removed the Holy Spirit from the book of Acts you would have nothing left.

Look at the deep conviction of the Spirit shown in today's text: 'When the people heard this, they were cut to the heart.' The scene in the second chapter of Acts is so different from that which we see in many churches today. We may be accustomed to hearing evangelists call people to be saved, but here the people are calling out to the evangelist, 'What must we do to be saved?' Such is the power of the Holy Spirit's conviction that they are 'cut to the heart'. How we long to see that same kind of empowering flowing through the Church today.

This raises a question: suppose there had been no Holy Spirit given on the Day of Pentecost, just what form would Christianity have taken? There would have been the message of the four Gospels without the life and power imparted on that day. The good news would have ended with the truth of the resurrection. But great though the resurrection was, and necessary in the divine scheme of things, clearly something else was needed to move people to cry out, 'What must we do to be saved?' That 'something else' was, of course, the Holy Spirit. At Pentecost, the same power that raised Christ from the dead (the Holy Spirit) raised 3,000 from the dead – that's 3,000 sinners who were dead in trespasses and sins!

FURTHER STUDY

John 14:15–31; 16:5–16

1. What did Jesus say the Holy Spirit would do?

2. What would He convict the world of?

Father, can it be that though the Holy Spirit is available to us in just the same way that He was to the Early Church, we do not allow Him the same freedom? If so, forgive us. And help us. In Jesus' name. Amen.

An ideal Christian meeting

'these people... have received the Holy Spirit just as we have.' (v47)

We continue reflecting on the truth that one of the great distinctives of the first-century Church was the empowering ministry of the Spirit. Look with me now as we explore how the Holy Spirit worked to bring Gentiles into the Church, which up to this moment was mainly Jewish.

When Cornelius, a Roman centurion, had been instructed by an angel to send for Peter, Peter receives a vision of a sheet let down from heaven containing all manner of beasts, reptiles, and birds, some of which Jews were forbidden to eat (Lev. 11). A voice tells him: 'Get up, Peter. Kill and eat' (v13). Peter refuses because it goes against his Jewish customs and belief. After the sheet has been lowered and raised three times, he sees the full significance of the words: not only is the distinction between clean and unclean food being abolished; so too is the distinction between 'clean' and 'unclean' people.

FURTHER STUDY

Rom. 2:25–29;
1 Cor. 12:13;
Gal. 3:26–29;
Col. 2:11–12

1. How does circumcision of the heart take place?

2. What is the result?

When Peter arrives at Cornelius' house, he finds himself in what has been described as an 'ideal Christian meeting'. First, it had an ideal chairman. Cornelius did not prevaricate but gave the kind of introduction every preacher would like to have: 'Now we are all here in the presence of God to listen to everything the Lord has commanded you to tell us' (v33). It had an ideal preacher also. Peter began 'telling the good news of peace through Jesus Christ' (v36). And it had, too, an ideal congregation who were eager and expectant, and as Peter spoke the Spirit came on them (v44). This perhaps highlights that if the Spirit is not at work in your church, don't necessarily look to the leader; it may be because the people are not expectant.

Holy God, I see how easy it is to paralyse a meeting of the Church simply by the lack of expectancy. When I gather with other believers may my spirit always be expectant, I pray. In Jesus' name. Amen.

'Refined ineffectuality'

FOR READING & MEDITATION – ACTS 19:1–7

'[Paul] asked them, "Did you receive the Holy Spirit when you believed?" They answered, "No"' (v2)

Two days ago we said that if Christianity had ended with the Gospels, it would have been a gospel without life and power – not a gospel that would conquer the world. The significance of the events recorded in the four Gospels had to be understood by Jesus' followers and conveyed to others in the power of the Holy Spirit.

In today's passage we see a Holy Spirit-less religion – good on facts and rules but lacking empowerment. When Paul arrived in Ephesus he sensed this lack in one group of disciples, and so his first question was, 'Did you receive the Holy Spirit when you believed?' They answered, 'No, we have not even heard that there is a Holy Spirit.' There were twelve in that group, and without the Holy Spirit what were they doing? Very little, it seems. They were just holding their own.

Apollos, when he came to Ephesus, was in a similar situation. Until instructed by Aquila and Priscilla, he was the picture of a present-day highly trained pastor who was eloquent and well-versed in Scripture (18:24–25). The result of theological training without the Holy Spirit is to produce what someone has termed 'refined ineffectuality'. Sadly, today there are pulpits occupied by people who have behind them years of training but no experience or dependence on the Spirit. The result? Refined ineffectuality and cultured emptiness.

What a difference between the 'twelve' at Ephesus and the other 'Twelve' – the twelve apostles. The other 'Twelve' were turning the world upside down; this 'twelve' were barely holding on. Training and refinement may be good but they are no substitute for the Holy Spirit and a God-dependent life.

FURTHER STUDY

Ezek. 36:26–30;
John 14:17;
Rom. 8:9;
1 Cor. 3:16

1. What had Ezekiel prophesied?

2. What did Jesus promise concerning the Holy Spirit?

Dear God, save us from this refined emptiness that makes Christianity a culture without conversion. Give us men and women who will stand in the pulpit and preach empowered by Your Spirit. In Jesus' name. Amen.

'This is what I am like'

FOR READING & MEDITATION – ACTS 17:1–9

'These men who have caused trouble all over the world have now come here' (v6)

Even a casual reader of Acts cannot help but be struck by the fact that Jesus Christ seems bigger and greater in the book of Acts (in terms of His miraculous and transforming power) than He does in the Gospels. Jesus on earth had great power, but Jesus in His Church is even more powerful. Jesus, working through the Holy Spirit, has enabled and empowered His people, as we see from today's text, to 'turn the world upside down' (v6, AV).

It is clear that, in many countries of the world, congregations are going back to the book of Acts for a fresh vision of the Church. One correspondent said, 'Our church has just gone through the Acts of the Apostles once again, and all our hearts are ashamed as we see how far we have drifted from the original pattern.' Is the Spirit leading His people back to His blueprint, we wonder? I cannot help but believe it. God is concerned that in every age He should have people on earth who show the world what He is really like. He longs to indwell us and empower us in this century in the same way that He empowered the Early Church. A Holy Spirit-less Christianity does nothing for anyone; nothing for the Church and nothing for the world.

FURTHER STUDY

John 15:16;
Acts 1:8; 4:1–13

1. What did the observers take note of?

2. What did Jesus say would happen when the Holy Spirit came on the disciples?

Perhaps the question we should ask ourselves is: are we as open to the energising and empowering ministry of the Spirit as were our brothers and sisters of the first century? Dr Harry Ironside, a pastor, said: 'In the Early Church the Holy Spirit was the pulse beat of all they did – the Life of their living. In the Church of [our] century sometimes it is difficult to find a pulse at all.'

Lord God, help us not to settle for anything less than the kind of power that energised Your Church in the Acts of the Apostles. Revive us, dear Lord, and bring us back to where you want us to be. In Jesus' name. Amen.

Feeding the mind

FOR READING & MEDITATION – ACTS 2:42–47

'They devoted themselves to the apostles' teaching' (v42)

Now we move on to explore another distinctive of the Early Church: their devotion to divine truth. In fact, several distinctives of the Early Church can be identified in the passage before us today. We shall look at the others later, but first we focus on the words 'They devoted themselves to the apostles' teaching...' Notice: they *devoted* themselves to it, which means that they gave it their undivided attention.

The first community of Christians was a learning and listening one. Clearly, the 3,000 new converts that came into the Church on the Day of Pentecost, plus the many others who were daily added to their number, gave themselves to listening to the apostles as they unfolded the truths concerning Jesus Christ, the Lord. They didn't gather to listen (as some may do today) with an attitude that says: 'I hope they won't go on too long this morning. I have quite a number of things I want to do before the start of next week.' And they did not become so taken up with the manifestations of the Spirit that they resented understanding the truth underpinning the miraculous. The Early Church, it seems, did not put intellectualism on a pedestal, but they were not anti-intellectual either.

FURTHER STUDY

John 5:31–40;
Acts 17:10–12;
Rom. 15:4

1. What was Jesus' indictment of the Jews?

2. What was the example of the Bereans?

One leader tells how he asked a man why he didn't go to church. In response the man said: 'Because every time I go to church I feel I have no need of anything above my collar. I might as well unscrew my head and put it under the seat!' That man, I think, would have been very comfortable in the Early Church. In my opinion he would have found not only inspiration for his heart but also food for his mind.

Father, You have given me a mind with which to think through the great issues of life, and I am deeply grateful for it. Help me become as devoted to divine truth as were those first disciples. In Jesus' name. Amen.

The only reliable doctrine

FOR READING & MEDITATION – 1 JOHN 2:18–27

'the anointing you received from him remains in you, and you do not need anyone to teach you.' (v27)

Today we digress slightly to look at a verse outside of the Acts of the Apostles; one which has a bearing on this matter of devotion to divine truth. One of the saddest things I know is to hear a Christian who has experienced a deep work of the Holy Spirit say something like this: 'Now that I am filled with the Spirit, He is the only teacher I need. I can dispense with all other teachers. The Spirit alone is my guide.' The text Christians sometimes use to support this position is the one before us today.

FURTHER STUDY

Psa. 71:17;
John 6:41–51;
Acts 18:24–25;
Eph. 4:21–24

1. Who is the supreme Teacher?

2. What is said of Apollos?

In this verse, John is not ruling out human teachers but is drawing attention to the problem caused by a group known as the Gnostics, or 'Knowing Ones', who influenced some of the Early Church. This sect propounded the idea that the teaching of the apostles was to be supplemented with the 'higher knowledge' they claimed to possess. John was saying that what the Christians had been taught under the Spirit's ministry through the apostles was not only adequate, but was also the only reliable doctrine. They needed nothing more than that they had received through the Spirit's unfolding of the apostles' teaching.

The teaching that has come down to us in the New Testament is the teaching of the apostles. When the canon (rule of faith) came to be fixed in the second, third and fourth centuries, the test of canonicity was whether a book had been written by the apostles or came with the authority of the apostles. Those who claim to be part of the Church but ignore or tamper with the apostles' doctrines are in error – plain and simple. Today's true followers will be like the Early Christians – 'devoted... to the apostles' teaching' (Acts 2:42).

God our Father, how can we sufficiently thank You for inspiring the first apostles to lay down for us the truths by which we, Your Church, are to operate? Help us not merely to believe them but to obey them. In Jesus' name. Amen.

At the apostles' feet

FOR READING & MEDITATION – ACTS 5:12–16

'And all the believers used to meet together in Solomon's Colonnade.'
(v12)

In order to get a feel of how important teaching was in the life of the Early Church, permit me to take you on an imaginary trip into that first Christian community.

We begin in one of the crowded homes in Jerusalem – crowded because many who were converted at Pentecost were visitors to the city, and a number stayed on in the homes of other Christians so that they might be grounded in the faith. Sometime after breakfast, everyone made their way to Solomon's Colonnade in the Temple. When they arrived, they sat on the floor with countless other believers to worship God and to understand the teaching of the apostles. There was no set schedule – just uninhibited worship, prayer and teaching, which probably lasted several hours.

FURTHER STUDY

1 Cor. 5:4;
Eph. 5:15–21;
Heb. 10:19–25

1. What did the writer of Hebrews exhort?

2. How are we to speak to one another?

Imagine how they would have felt as they heard Peter or Matthew or John describe all the things they had seen Jesus do and explain the words that He had said, and picture their faces as they listened spellbound to the amazing truths these men unfolded. One moment they might have rocked with laughter as one of the apostles said something humorous, and the next they might have wept as they heard again the grim details of Christ's death on the cross. Their time would probably have ended in quiet contemplation as they considered the consequences of their new-found faith. Then they would return to their homes to continue in fellowship and discussion.

This portrayal may give us an idea of Church life in the beginning. However, we can still sit at the apostles' feet as we open the inspired Word they have left us.

God my Father, give me an ever-growing appetite for divine truth, I pray, for I know that without it I cannot develop as a Christian. The entrance of Your Word gives light – and also life. I am deeply grateful. Amen.

The best training ground

FOR READING & MEDITATION – ACTS 7:1–16

'Brothers and fathers, listen to me!' (v2)

Today's reading shows that Stephen, who was a deacon, was obviously a gifted teacher too. He was chosen for his spiritual qualities (6:1–6), and his knowledge and grasp of Scripture as demonstrated in his sermon to the Sanhedrin is quite astonishing. Where did he get that knowledge and understanding? He got it, I imagine, first by studying the Scriptures for himself, but also by sitting at the apostles' feet, listening to their teaching.

Let's take another imaginary trip back to the days of the Early Church. Once again, picture yourself sitting in the large congregation that met in Solomon's Colonnade. Look around – who do you see? There's Stephen, Philip, Simeon, and over there is Agabus and an enthusiastic young convert named Silas. You will definitely be hearing from these men in the future, but not for a while. Despite the fact that it is a power-packed church, no one is going anywhere just yet – not even the apostles. In truth, it will be several years before the names I have mentioned come into prominence. They will one day have responsibility – great responsibility – but their main task right now is to experience daily the life of Christ as it is being worked out in His Church.

FURTHER STUDY

Col. 2:6–7;
2 Tim. 2:1–15;
Titus 1:9

1. What did Paul exhort Timothy to do?

2. What is one of the qualifications of an elder?

Men and women of God are often best prepared for future service by being involved in church life. Bible colleges are both helpful and important, but they are no substitute for serving Christ in the community of the Church. When you meet the people mentioned above a few years ahead, they will be towering spiritual giants. They were shaped by true Christian community – the best training ground there is.

Father, I must ask myself how willing I am to be shaped by the community in which You have put me. Give me a teachable and responsive spirit, I pray. In Jesus' name. Amen.

Building 'God's New Society' for generations to come

Gifts left in wills, large or small, are a wonderful way to support a cause you care about and make a lasting difference. CWR's ministry continues to grow and develop due to the generosity of all our supporters.

Many people who support the work of CWR often express their desire to give more. They recognise that this would enable us to reach many more with the gospel of Jesus.

'Leaving a gift to CWR in our will makes sense! We believe in CWR's work and have the opportunity to help. We have supported CWR for years and want to continue to do so in the future.'

By leaving a gift in your will to CWR, you will help secure the future of the ministry for years to come, by:
· Providing vital Christian books and resources for the next generation
· Supporting the training of counsellors with a Christian world-view
· Enabling free resources to be sent into prisons across the world
· Opening new doors in Asia by translating our books and materials into multiple languages
· Developing events and seminar programmes for churches and Christian groups to encourage and inspire their faith

To find out more about leaving a gift to CWR in your will, please call Amanda Pickering on **01252 784729**, or contact us on **legacy@cwr.org.uk**

Slow but sure

FOR READING & MEDITATION – ACTS 7:17–43

'[Moses] received living words to pass on to us.' (v38)

We continue reading through Stephen's sermon to the Sanhedrin in order to grasp something of the depth of his biblical knowledge and understanding. What a powerful sermon it was. Stephen, Philip, Simeon, Agabus, and many others – who were not apostles – grew to great spiritual stature by experiencing and serving Jesus in His Church. Before these people were given any responsibility in the Church they, like us all, went through the stages of just new to the faith life, rejoicing in their salvation, fellowshipping with other believers, and sitting at the feet of the apostles in order to understand more fully God's purpose for their lives. Though we made this point yesterday, it bears repeating: you simply cannot find anything more effective for producing top quality servants of God than ordinary church life – being the people of God in community.

FURTHER STUDY

Col. 1:3–11;
2 Thess. 1:3

1. What did Paul pray for the Colossians?

2. What did he give thanks for in relation to the Thessalonians?

It concerns me when I see organisations pick out promising young believers from a church and, after only a few weeks in the Christian life, thrust them into frontline activity. I fear they don't fully understand what they are doing. They are potentially robbing them of the joy of slow spiritual growth and maturity. The idea some Christians have is that everything in the book of Acts happened in the space of about two years. Stephen probably preached his famous sermon to the Sanhedrin about three years after Pentecost, and the first missionary journey took place about seventeen years after that great event! The Jerusalem believers were gradually, over time, equipped to live as God desired for them. They grew organically, steadily – the best way to grow.

Father, in an age when everything has to be 'instant', thank You for showing me the importance of slow growth. I want my life to be proven in the midst of church life. May this happen, I pray. In Jesus' name. Amen.

Another urgent need

FOR READING & MEDITATION – ACTS 5:17–25

'Look! The men you put in jail are standing in the temple courts teaching the people.' (v25)

The Early Church, as we are seeing, was a Church devoted to the apostles' teaching. Those first Christians were eager to learn and gave themselves wholeheartedly to the task of assimilating the truth and principles expounded by the apostles.

The apostles' teaching has come down to us in its definitive form into what we now call the New Testament. These days, when there are so many different opinions and views being promoted in our churches, one of the most urgent needs is to recover an understanding of the authority of the apostles. When the apostles taught in the early years of the Church, they knew that Jesus had given them a unique authority, and the Church that existed in the period immediately after the apostles knew it also. Ignatius, bishop of the church at Antioch who was martyred about AD 110 had, according to tradition, heard the apostles and may have been ordained by Peter or Paul. However, he wrote: 'I do not issue you with commands like Peter or Paul for I am not an apostle.' He was a bishop, but not an apostle, and he knew that he did not have the authority to issue commands as did the apostles.

FURTHER STUDY

Rom. 10:1–13;
2 Cor. 4:1–6;
2 Tim. 4:2

1. What did Paul proclaim?

2. What was Paul's charge to Timothy?

What is tragic about some sections of today's Church is that they have lost a sense of biblical authority. Consequently, no clear message flows out from many modern pulpits. A true New Testament church is a biblical church – a church that believes the Bible, understands the Bible, teaches the Bible, and lives according to the Bible. Where the Bible is not opened, the Church speaks with a stutter. It may express opinions, but really, without the authority of the Bible, it adds little to life today.

Lord God, bring Your Church back once again to Your Word. Show us how that without the Scriptures we have no real authority. Save us from stuttering and help us to speak with a clear voice. Indeed, with one voice. In Jesus' name we pray. Amen.

Real community

FOR READING & MEDITATION – 1 JOHN 1:1–10

*'But if we walk in the light, as he is in the light, we have fellowship
with one another'* (v7)

Now we move on to think about another distinctive of the
Early Church: a rich sense of community and fellowship.
Immediately after Pentecost we read, 'They devoted themselves
to the apostles' teaching *and to the fellowship*' (Acts 2:42,
emphasis added).

As you may already know, the Greek word for 'fellowship'
is *koinonia* (pronounced 'coinownia'). This word can also be
translated 'community' – and implies living together as one
family in deep, rich and authentic relationships, and having
things in common. The coming of the Holy Spirit
produced in the lives of the early Christians a spirit
of oneness and unity that was quite remarkable.
Prior to Pentecost there was no real identifiable
sense of fellowship among God's people. There was
friendship, consideration, even love, but no deep
sense of unity and oneness. As the Holy Spirit was
living in them they were drawn together into the
kind of fellowship that cannot be achieved in any
other way. Once we belong to Jesus, we belong to
everyone else who belongs to Jesus.

**FURTHER
STUDY**

1 John 2:7–11;
3:11–24

1. What is the
basis of our
fellowship
together?

2. What is the
demonstration
of it?

Perhaps we do not have the same concept of
fellowship as did the Early Church. Today, generally speaking,
the word 'fellowship' is used to describe a genial get-together
of Christians, followed by coffee and biscuits. Have you
ever wondered how the Early Church managed to do so
much without coffee and biscuits? Please don't think I am
opposing life groups or socialising. I am simply saying that
koinonia goes far beyond that and is much deeper and much
richer. May the Lord help us to redeem the word and, in our
churches, live in true fellowship just as the Early Church did.

**Father, help me to understand that without *koinonia* the Church is
not at its best. We live well only when we are in fellowship –
fellowship with You and with each other. Make us participants in
true *koinonia*. For Jesus' sake we pray. Amen.**

'In constant review'

FOR READING & MEDITATION – GALATIANS 2:1–10

'James, Peter and John... gave me and Barnabas the right hand of fellowship' (v9)

Yesterday we commented that sadly some Church communities lack the rich, deep fellowship experienced by the first-century Christians. Anyone who reads the Acts of the Apostles will almost instantly realise that there is a world of difference between the way the Early Church lived and the way we live today. 'It is the depravity of institutions,' observes one author, 'that given in the beginning to express life, they often end in throttling that very life. Therefore they need constant review, perpetual criticism, a continuous bringing back to the original purpose and spirit.' You may feel, as you read day by day through these current meditations, that they are unnecessarily harsh but, believe me, behind them is much tenderness and sadness that we aren't living in the good of all that God desires, according to the original blueprint for His Church and His children. In attempting to live in Christian community, in its original purpose and spirit, we as His ambassadors and representatives need to be able to continually and honestly review our relationship and daily walk with God and each other.

FURTHER STUDY

Acts 2:22–47;
1 Cor. 2:2; 9:16;
2 Cor. 4:5

1. What did Peter present?

2. What happened as a result?

A minister once told me about a group of Christian students at a particular university who carried out a survey of what their fellow students thought about Christ and the Church. The students were first asked to give an opinion on how they viewed Christ, and then on how they viewed the Church. Afterwards, when they analysed the survey, the Christian students got a shock. They found that only 5% of those questioned were for the Church, yet 85% said they were for Christ. Let's pray that Jesus will be free to reign in His Church.

Father, help us to be honest with You and each other. Help us see that one of the reasons why Jesus died was so that His followers could enjoy true fellowship and communion. Please enable us to understand this. In Jesus' name. Amen.

Sharing in and sharing out

FOR READING & MEDITATION – PHILIPPIANS 2:1–18

*'If you have any encouragement from being united with Christ...
if any fellowship with the Spirit' (v1)*

Today we continue focusing on the word *koinonia* in order to try to understand more of its meaning. *Koinonia*, as we said, means partnership or fellowship, and it is a fellowship in which all are equal. C.H. Dodd, a Greek scholar, explains: 'The noun *Koinonia* means fellowship, *Koinonos* (another noun) means partner, and the verb *Koinoneo* means to share.' From this we can see that those who partake in the *koinonia* share in a common concern. But what is it that we share?

First, we share in the same inheritance – rescued from the kingdom of darkness and brought into the kingdom of light, receiving a restored relationship with our heavenly Father, redeemed by the blood of the same Son, and indwelt by the presence of the same Holy Spirit. The same God who lives in me lives in you. The same blood that saved me also saved you. The same Spirit who empowers my life is also in you. This makes us one family.

Koinonia is something we share in together, but it is also something we share out. *Koinonia* has to do not only with what we possess, but what we do with what we possess. So what do we share with one another? We share everything God wants us to share. In the days immediately following Pentecost, Christians in Jerusalem were called to share their possessions with one another and to have everything in common. There were particular circumstances that required this; for example, the vast number of pilgrims who came to Christ at Pentecost who made their home in Jerusalem. Although God may not call us to do the same thing today, this question remains: are we willing and if He did, would we?

FURTHER STUDY

Acts 10:34–35;
Gal. 3:28;
James 2:1–17

1. What does it mean to show favouritism?

2. How is this overcome by true fellowship?

Father, help me in all honesty to answer this question. If self-interest has a strong hold on me then dissolve it by the power of Your love I pray. In Jesus' name. Amen.

God-dependency

FOR READING & MEDITATION – EPHESIANS 4:1–16

'until we all reach unity in the faith and in the knowledge of the Son of God' (v13)

As we read Acts we can see that the Early Church enjoyed a degree of community and relationship that was greater than anything ever known before. At least four aspects of this unity can be observed in the Church that was established on the day of Pentecost.

The first unity, of course, was unity with God. If there is no unity with God then disharmony spreads itself all down the line of human relationships. The first Christians were so God-dependent that they took on the significance of the one on whom they were dependent. The consciousness that God is working in and through you, thinking in and through you, is one of the greatest annulments of inferiority and fear that I know. 'In Him who strengthens me, I am able for anything,' said Paul (Phil. 4:13, Moffatt). God-dependence is a humbling experience, but it is also a Hallelujah experience.

A second unity was unity among themselves. Doubtless there were many strong personalities in the Early Church who were well able to express themselves, but in the atmosphere of the Spirit, self-centredness gives way to other-centredness. No one was more given to individualistic self-expression than Peter. That's why I love the verse that says, 'Then Peter stood up with the Eleven' (Acts 2:14). Previously he had often stood against the Eleven, but now he was with them and alongside them. When he spoke, the Eleven spoke in him and through him. They were one with each other and spoke with one voice. A 'good Christian' was once described as 'one who gets along well with others according to Jesus Christ'. How many of us, I wonder (myself included), can be described this way?

FURTHER STUDY

1 Cor. 1:9;
Eph. 4:1–32;
1 John 1:7

1. What causes disunity?

2. How can we grow up together?

Father, help me understand that unity is not something I create; You have already created it through Christ and the Holy Spirit. Help us to stop trying to make unity, and simply surrender to it. In Jesus' name. Amen.

The results of unity

FOR READING & MEDITATION – PSALM 133:1–3

'How good and pleasant it is when brothers live together in unity!'
(v1)

Yesterday we thought about two aspects of the unity created by the Holy Spirit which became so clear in the Early Church after Pentecost. A third unity was one we have already touched upon: unity in their attitude to material possessions. 'All the believers were together and had everything in common' (Acts 2:44). The unity of the Spirit resulted in a unity of economic interests and goods. Today some Christians attempt to create the *koinonia* by getting together in a community and voluntarily sharing their possessions. But sharing possessions was not the cause of *koinonia* – it was the result of it. I do not doubt that God does call some people to live in community, but whether or not He calls you to do this, every one of us needs to be open to His prompting to share what we have with others.

FURTHER STUDY

Acts 20:32–38;
2 Cor. 9:6;
Gal. 6:10

1. What were Paul's farewell words to the Ephesian elders?

2. What did he remind the Corinthians of?

A fourth unity was a unity of all people, regardless of race or culture. Admittedly, at first the Early Church revealed its prejudice – it took a vision from heaven to get Peter to go to the Gentiles – but eventually the Spirit prevailed. Look at this: 'In the church at Antioch there were prophets and teachers: Barnabas, Simeon called Niger' (13:1). Simeon is widely thought to be an African gentile and held an important position and ministry gifts which he exercised in the church at Antioch. Along with others, he laid his hands on Barnabas and Paul to send them out to preach the gospel (13:3). Gentile, Jew, African, Asian, rich or poor, whole or broken, God has opened the gates of His kingdom wide for all to enter and He has made His Church the welcome committee. Our prejudice and preferences have been superseded by God's heart of love for all.

Lord God, show us how we can restore this fourfold unity to the Church of the twenty-first century. You are not withholding Your Spirit – but are we withholding ours? If we are, please forgive us and help us. In Jesus' name. Amen.

The Church as bread

FOR READING & MEDITATION – 1 CORINTHIANS 10:14–33

'Because there is one loaf, we, who are many, are one body' (v17)

While considering the *koinonia* of the Early Church, we ought to acknowledge another phrase found in Acts 2:42: 'They devoted themselves to the apostles' teaching... to the fellowship, *to the breaking of bread...'*

The term 'breaking of bread' is almost certainly a reference to what we now call the Lord's Supper or Holy Communion. At first the believers would celebrate their oneness in Christ over a meal, and at the same time remember the cause of that oneness – Jesus' death at Calvary. They would break open a loaf and pass it to each other, giving thanks to God as they did so for their unity in Christ. We know from Paul's first letter to the Corinthians that within a short period of time some Christians became more interested in eating than in celebrating their unity in Christ (1 Cor. 11:17–34). This prompted the apostle to lay down new guidelines for celebrating the Lord's Supper. The breaking of one loaf, practised by the Early Church, was meant to underline their unity as one Body.

A loaf of bread is a fitting figure of the unity of the Church for at least four reasons. First, bread is a unity made up of many units. Second, it is the product of both earth and heaven. Earth produces the grain, but it needs rain from heaven to water it. Third, bread, like the Church, is not a luxury, but a necessity. We can manage without cake, but bread is a staple food. Fourth, bread can only fulfil its function through fraction. It is made to be broken. The Church, like bread, is to be broken in God's hands if it is to be of service to the world. All this, and more, was caught up in the simple but sacred act of the breaking of bread.

FURTHER STUDY

Matt. 5:23–24; 26:26;
1 Cor. 11:17–34

1. What happens when we disregard the Lord's table?

2. How does 'examination' relate to 'unity'?

Father, I am grateful for all that I receive when I draw near to the communion table, but may the wonder of the unity of Your body come home to me, too, when I draw near to my own dining table. In Jesus' name I ask it. Amen.

Is Church life dangerous?

FOR READING & MEDITATION – 1 CORINTHIANS 11:17–22

'I have no praise for you, for your meetings do more harm than good.'
(v17)

Having seen something of the deep sense of community and fellowship that existed in the Early Church, we must now ask the question: to what extent is first church *koinonia* reflected in the Church today? Generally speaking, possibly because twenty-first-century life is difficult to compare with the early Church situation, it's a difficult question to answer. While there is love, friendliness and sharing in Christian churches, when measured against the *koinonia* of the New Testament – the commitment to share each other's lives in the deepest way possible – today's Church seems a little lacklustre.

FURTHER STUDY

Prov. 11:30;
Matt. 4:19;
1 Cor. 9:1–27

1. How did Paul seek to win people?

2. How does this demonstrate *koinonia*?

Please note that I am generalising, for there will be many exceptions to what I am saying here. However, as a first-hand observer of church life for many years, I am compelled to say that when it comes to true *koinonia*, many churches fall short of the ideal. 'Going to some churches,' says one writer, 'can be dangerous to your health.' He continues: 'I have the scars to prove it. But you can't see them at the front. They're all at the back!' Another disillusioned Christian said, 'I found more understanding and compassion in the world than I did in the Church.'

While we thank God for those churches where true *koinonia* functions, there are far too many where backbiting, gossip, cliquishness and lack of consideration for others rules the day. How sad it is that in so many places God is worshipped and the Word of God is preached but *koinonia* is conspicuous by its absence. There is no doubt in my mind that the nearest thing to heaven on earth is a fellowship of Christians who are living in true community and relating to one another in the Spirit of Jesus Christ.

God my Father, help us, Your present-day Church, into a living fellowship which transcends all race and class, and to know a unity that the Church enjoyed in its beginnings. Amen.

Praying and shaking

FOR READING & MEDITATION – ACTS 4:23–31

'they raised their voices together in prayer to God.' (v24)

Moving on, we now look at another distinctive of the Early Church: the practice of persevering, faithful prayer. The book of Acts contains many accounts of how believers turned to prayer when they found themselves in difficulty. But their prayers were not just limited to times of emergency only; often they prayed for a long time just for the joy of developing their relationship with their loving heavenly Father.

This latter aspect of prayer – praying for the sheer pleasure of communicating with heaven – is, I believe, what is being conveyed in Acts 2:42: 'They devoted themselves to the apostles' teaching and to the fellowship, to the breaking of bread *and to prayer*' (emphasis added). We should never forget that the Church was born in a prayer meeting, and I am convinced that to those early believers it was unthinkable that they could ever grow spiritually without recourse to prayer.

FURTHER STUDY

John 17:1–26;
Acts 10:1–4

1. How did Jesus model prayer?

2. What is said of Cornelius?

Look again at today's reading: Peter and John had been before the Sanhedrin and had been commanded not to speak any more in the name of Jesus (v18). So when they are released what do they do? They go back to their fellow Christians, report the facts – and pray. What might we have prayed for under the same circumstances? That the minds of the members of the Sanhedrin might be changed? But listen to their request: 'Enable your servants to speak your word with great boldness' (v29). How did God answer their prayer? We read, 'the place where they were meeting was shaken' (v31). It was as if God was saying, 'Don't be afraid; let me show you how much power is at my disposal.' It certainly worked, for we then read, 'they were all filled with the Holy Spirit and spoke the word of God boldly' (v31).

Dear God, wake us up to the power that is available to us through persevering faithful prayer. We know this in theory, but we are so reluctant to give ourselves unreservedly to such prayer. Forgive us and help us. In Jesus' name we ask it. Amen.

CWR Summer School is back!

In previous years, CWR has hosted a Summer School, enabling visitors from both the UK and overseas to come and experience our world-renowned teaching amidst the amazing setting of Waverley Abbey House. Previous guests who visited summer schools have since been called into church and charity leadership, been equipped to help others in pastoral roles, and begun transforming works overseas.

So we are excited to be able to once again offer a week here at Waverley, during which you can meet and sit under the teaching of our experienced team of tutors, enjoy the fellowship of many others who have a heart to see God's Word read and applied in their lives, be looked after by our incredible hospitality team, and also enjoy times of fun, recreation, creativity and fellowship.

The week will run from the morning of Monday 15 July right through until the afternoon of Saturday 20 July, with an option to stay overnight at Waverley on Sunday 14 July for those travelling a distance to join us. A range of options on seminars, accommodation and dietary requirement will cater for all your tastes and needs.

So we're very pleased to invite you to join us for a week of fellowship and life-transforming teaching from CWR tutors Mick Brooks, Lynette Brooks, Philip Greenslade, Bob Stradling, Andy Peck and others, as well as guest contributors including Carl Beech. Here is just a selection of the topics and activities available:

Seminars

Christ Empowered Living
Great Chapters of the Bible
Spiritual Direction
Mental Health and the Church
Bringing the Bible to Life
Mentoring

Activities

Choir workshop
Communion in the Abbey ruins
Worship and devotional times
A celebratory evening banquet
Bread making
A BBQ in the grounds
Fellowship with the CWR team
... and much more!

There are also options for evening seminars, two and three-day non-residential options, so do check out all the details on our website for prices and ticketing options. But do hurry – spaces are filling fast!

For more information, visit **cwr.org.uk/summerschool**

'He is praying'

FOR READING & MEDITATION – ACTS 9:1–19

'ask for a man from Tarsus named Saul, for he is praying.' (v11)

We continue looking at this important aspect of prayer in the Early Church. One of the great characters of Acts is the apostle Paul. Above everything else he was a praying man, and the way in which his prayer life began is quite intriguing.

Paul (or Saul as he was known at first) was struck down and blinded when Jesus appeared to him on the Damascus Road. He who had laid many low was now himself laid low. 'For three days he was blind,' says the record, 'and did not eat or drink anything' (v9). What did he do during those three sightless days? He prayed. The fact that Saul, who had been bent on destroying the Church, was now praying to the one whose purposes he had tried to frustrate is surely incredible. But amazing as it may be to us, imagine how astonished Ananias must have been when God told him to go and lay hands of healing on the very man who had been coming to lay hands of destruction on him. Yet he obeys. Saul of Tarsus had lost his physical vision, but he gained a new spiritual vision. As he wrote in Ephesians 1:18, the eyes of his heart were gloriously opened.

Paul, who without doubt became one of the greatest prayer warriors of all time, instinctively prayed from his conversion. Granted, his conversion was powerful and dramatic, but it's important to emphasise that one of the very best things that those new to faith can do is develop their new relationship with God, and that is the primary purpose of prayer. Where and how we learn to pray is not important; what is important is that we do it, for without prayer there is only a stuttering and stilted march of progress in the Christian life.

FURTHER STUDY

Rom. 1:9–10;
Eph. 1:15–23;
Phil. 1:9–11;
Col. 1:9–14

1. What is a hallmark of Paul's letters?

2. What are some of the things he prays for?

My Father and my God, let this note go ringing through my soul today: my prayer moments are my greatest moments. Help me to remember that prayer is the Christian's vital breath. In Jesus' name. Amen.

Locked in and locked out

FOR READING & MEDITATION – ACTS 12:1–19

*'[Rhoda] exclaimed, "Peter is at the door!" "You're out of your mind,"
they told her.' (vv14–15)*

Today we look in on one of the great prayer meetings
of history – a prayer meeting that brought about the
deliverance of Peter from prison.

Herod had already put James to death (v2), and now no
doubt it was his intention to do the same to Peter also. When
some of the Christians in Jerusalem heard that Peter had been
imprisoned, they immediately went to the house of Mary, the
mother of Mark, and began to pray. Their prayer was sincere,
earnest and 'without ceasing' (v5, AV) and God answered by
sending an angel into the prison to expedite Peter's
escape. Imagine Peter's surprise when a light shines
into his cell, the chains fall off his wrists, and the
angel says to him: 'Quick, get up!… Put on your
clothes and sandals… and follow me' (vv7–8). They
reach the main gate of the prison, which opens up of
its own accord – just like an automatic door. When
Peter is well outside the prison and is able to manage
on his own, the angel leaves him.

Immediately he makes his way to the house of
Mary and knocks at the outer door. Rhoda, the
servant girl who answers, recognises Peter's voice,
but she is so excited that she runs back into the house,
forgetting to open the door! Peter has to knock repeatedly before
he is finally let in. The apostle seemed to have more trouble
getting into the prayer meeting than he did in getting out of
prison! It's not unusual that when Christians gather together
to pray they are surprised to find that God actually answers
our prayers. Unusual, and yet quite usual! I'm extremely glad
God hears and answers those prayers that so often are mixed
with unexpectancy and doubt.

**FURTHER
STUDY**

Isa. 58:9;
65:17–25;
Jer. 33:3;
Rom. 10:12

1. What had
God promised?

2. How do we
know these
promises are for
all who believe?

**Father, I am so grateful that You answer my prayers even when You
know that I am going to react with amazement and surprise when
Your answer comes. Thank You for Your steadfast love and
faithfulness. Where would I be without it? Amen.**

The Church goes 'catholic'

FOR READING & MEDITATION – ACTS 13:1–12

'So after they had fasted and prayed, they placed their hands on them and sent them off.' (v3)

Another amazing moment in Acts that is surrounded by an atmosphere of faithful prayer is the commissioning of Barnabas and Saul for the work of the ministry. The whole history of Western civilisation was redirected in that hour, for out of that hour went two men who gave the gospel to Europe – and to us. This is the section of Acts that tells us how the Church became catholic, and by 'catholic' I mean 'universal'; for everyone without distinction.

Five men in the church at Antioch – Barnabas, Simeon, Lucius, Manaen and Saul (Paul) – met together to fast and worship God. As they did so, the Holy Spirit spoke to them, indicating that He had a special work to do through Barnabas and Saul. A good deal of discussion has taken place down the centuries on just how the Holy Spirit got His message across to these five praying men. Some say it must have come through the voice of one of the prophets; others say one of the teachers would have conveyed it. Still others believe it would have come as a distinct impression to all five of them at the same time. Scripture is silent on the issue, but what is clear is this: once the Spirit had made known His will, they continued to fast and pray.

FURTHER STUDY

Luke 11:1–10; Acts 16:1–10

1. How was Jesus' promise fulfilled?

2. What was the result?

How committed these early disciples were to be waiting before God in patient prayer. If this same situation occurred in today's Church, upon hearing the Spirit's voice we would no doubt rise to take immediate action. These believers, however, sensed that Barnabas and Saul were about to enter a historic moment, and they needed to be sure everything they did was in tune with the will of God. We would do well to remember that sometimes hasty action is worse than no action.

Father, teach me how to take every step in the atmosphere of patient prayer. And save me from doing everything in a rush. Slow me down, dear Lord, that I might keep pace with Your purposes. In Jesus' name. Amen.

Power breaks through

FOR READING & MEDITATION – ROMANS 12:9–21

'Be... faithful in prayer.' (v12)

Over the past few days we have been seeing how important the practice of persistent, faithful prayer was to the Early Church. The Church, we said at the beginning of these meditations, was born in a prayer meeting, and on almost every page of the Acts of the Apostles, both individually and corporately, believers are seen to be at prayer.

It would not be true to say that the twenty-first-century Church has stopped believing in the power of prayer, but it could be true to say that we are not as good as the Early Church at practising it. Many churches report that the least attended meeting in the church programme is the prayer meeting. It might sound a simplistic observation to some, but in my opinion the main reason why some churches today do not experience the same degree of empowering in their life as did the Early Church is because it does not give the same amount of time to prayer.

FURTHER STUDY

1 Chron. 16:11;
Matt. 26:41;
Luke 18:1–8;
John 16:24

1. What is Jesus' teaching in this parable?

2. How did Jesus chide the disciples?

Over the years I have asked myself this question many times: at what point does the power of God break through into the life of the Church? The only conclusion I can come to is this: it breaks through at the point of prayer. God's empowering surges like a mighty ocean just waiting to find a point at which it can break through into the life of every Christian community. But the only point where it can break through is the point of prayer. When we pray a little then a little of God's power breaks through; when we pray a lot then a lot of His power breaks through. It is as simple as that. One preacher put it like this: 'It is not that prayer has been tried and found wanting. It is rather that it has not really been tried.'

Lord God, show me again that the reason why You want Your Church to pray is not to bring Your purposes in line with ours, but to bring our purposes in line with Yours. Forgive us that we so easily forget that. In Jesus' name. Amen.

The key doctrine

FOR READING & MEDITATION – ACTS 2:22–41

'God has made this Jesus, whom you crucified, both Lord and Christ.'
(v36)

Yet another distinctive of the Early Church that we discover in the Acts of the Apostles is the emphasis which the believers placed on the lordship of Christ. Did you know that there are over a hundred references in the book of Acts to the lordship of Jesus Christ? The prominence given to this theme indicates that this is an issue of tremendous spiritual importance. John Stott, in a sermon he gave one year at the Keswick Convention, said: 'If I were to ask you what is the master key doctrine in the Scriptures, I wonder what you would answer? The sovereignty of God? The cross? The fullness of the Spirit? I would argue that the master key is... the lordship of Christ.' I agree.

FURTHER STUDY

Rom. 14:9;
1 Cor. 8:1–6;
12:3;
1 Pet. 3:21–22

1. What does the Holy Spirit enable us to declare?

2. How does Peter describe Christ's lordship?

Peter's sermon to the crowd gathered on the Day of Pentecost is punctuated with references to the lordship of Christ, and this is the point he highlights in today's text: 'God has made this Jesus, whom you crucified, both Lord and Christ.' You see, no one can become a disciple of Christ, or continue to be a disciple of Christ, unless they give themselves to Christ's lordship. There are some who claim that it is possible for us to take Jesus as Saviour at the moment of our conversion and then receive Him as Lord at a later stage when we decide to give to Him our all. This is not biblical teaching. The recognition that Jesus Christ is God (and therefore Lord of all) is the one and only door into salvation. We could never have been saved by the intervention of a created being, such as an angel. It took God to save us. And without this admission – that Jesus is the Lord – there is simply no way into the kingdom of God.

Lord God, thank You for finding a way to restore our broken relationship. Once again I give my life to You. Be Lord in my life. May Your will be done and Your kingdom come in me today. In Jesus' name. Amen.

A shock to the system

FOR READING & MEDITATION – ACTS 22:1–16

*'"Who are you, Lord?" I asked. "I am Jesus of Nazareth,
whom you are persecuting," he replied.' (v8)*

Focusing still on the theme of the lordship of Jesus, we look
once again at the conversion of Saul of Tarsus. Ponder this
question: what was it that put Saul off his food for three days
and overturned his theology?

I am slightly amused at the different ways in which great
thinkers and philosophers over the years have tried to explain
the reason for Saul's discomfiture on the Damascus Road. One
suggests that he had an epileptic seizure. This is what he says:
'Saul, who later became Paul, was an epileptic visionary who
used his physical problems to spiritual ends.' Well,
all I can say in response is that Saul, the 'epileptic
visionary', has enabled more clarity and wholeness
to a greater number of people than any man who
ever lived – save only Jesus. One theologian suggests
that what unsettled him was a lightning flash
which he mistook for a revelation from heaven. 'We
all know what happens to people when struck by
lightning,' he says. 'They are disoriented for days.'
I feel both sad and angry when I hear so-called
scholars trivialising the conversion of the great
apostle Paul. He who has been instrumental in
converting multitudes – was his conversion unreal?

**FURTHER
STUDY**
John 10:4;
18:37;
Acts 9:1–19;
Rev. 1:15

1. Who was Paul
persecuting?
2. What impact
did the voice of
Christ have?

The thing, so I believe, that had such a profound effect upon
Saul of Tarsus was not the blinding light but the illumination
that came to his soul concerning Jesus of Nazareth. Previously
he thought that Jesus was just a carpenter from Nazareth;
now he saw that He was none other than the Lord of the
universe. It was a shock to both his spiritual and physical
systems. But he came through it to be the greatest advocate
of Christ's lordship that the world has ever seen.

**Father, I am so thankful for the way You brought Paul into Your
kingdom and for the fact that his blazing heart has set others on
fire. Set me on fire also so that I too can kindle a flame of love for
You in others. Amen.**

The glorious ascension

FOR READING & MEDITATION – ACTS 1:6–11

'he was taken up before their very eyes, and a cloud hid him from their sight.' (v9)

We pause in our meditations for a couple of days to consider Jesus' ascension. Although the Christian Church has celebrated Ascension Day (the sixth Thursday after Easter) for many centuries, there are those (sceptics and liberals) who regard the ascension of Jesus to heaven as nothing more than a graphic myth or a triumphalist parable. Accepting as I do the full authority and veracity of Scripture, I believe that what we read about in today's passage – the ascension of our Lord to glory – is a definite fact and one of the great cardinal truths of the Christian faith.

FURTHER STUDY

Mark 16:19;
Luke 24:51;
Heb. 4:14;
9:23–28

1. How did the writer of Hebrews describe the ascension?

2. Why is Christ's ascension so crucial?

Ian Macpherson said that the New Testament represents the ascension as a sublime drama in three acts: secession, procession and accession. By secession he means the withdrawal of Christ from the earth. Jesus not only had to leave the earth, He had to be seen to leave it. If Jesus had walked over the Mount of Olives and disappeared from sight, the disciples might have expected Him to reappear as He had during the previous 40 days. His ascension from the Mount of Olives made it clear that He would not do so. A wider and greater ministry awaited Him.

The ascension, however, involved not only a secession but also a procession. Listen to this: 'When he ascended on high, he led captives in his train and gave gifts to men' (Eph. 4:8). Jesus, when He passed into heaven, had behind Him a train of defeated adversaries – probably the spiritual enemies who were overcome at the cross.

Then to secession and procession we must add accession. Jesus remember, ascended to a throne and sits there now at the right hand of God – King of kings and Lord of lords.

Risen, exalted and glorified Lord, I see that Your ascension meant that You went from the here to the everywhere – although out of our sight, but nearer to our hearts. Thank You, dear Saviour. Amen.

A ten-day prayer meeting

FOR READING & MEDITATION – ACTS 1:12–26

'They all joined together constantly in prayer' (v14)

After Jesus had been taken up to heaven, the apostles returned to Jerusalem to await the 'promise of the Father' (v4, RSV). All the apostles were there except Judas, who by this time had gone to where he belonged (v25). The selection of an apostle to fill the vacancy left by Judas took place by lot (v26), and there has been much debate over the years as to whether or not this was the correct move. Some theologians think the disciples were rather hasty in choosing Matthias and should have waited a little longer. Had they done so they would have been able to include the apostle Paul as the twelfth member of the group. Those who counter this view suggest that the fact that Peter quoted from the book of Psalms suggests that he could not have been wrong in his understanding of the situation.

Important though the selection of a new apostle was, a matter of equal significance is recorded in this passage: the apostles, together with over a hundred of Christ's followers, 'joined together constantly in prayer'. We in the Christian Church tend to make much of the day of Pentecost (and rightly so), but often we overlook what happened in the ten days between the ascension and Pentecost. This, remember, was the first time the 'believers' had met together after Jesus had returned to heaven – and they met together to pray. Mary the mother of Jesus was there, we are told (v14). Isn't it interesting that the last glimpse we have of the mother of Jesus is at a prayer meeting! She who had carried the Saviour in her womb – her gift to the world – was now waiting to be filled with the Spirit – His gift to her.

FURTHER STUDY

Acts 4:23–31; 12:5,11–12; 16:13–15; 21:5

1. What was the pattern of the Early Church?

2. What were some of the results?

Father, I know that all great movements begin in prayer. But are things not being brought to birth because we, Your people, lack both persistence and power in prayer? Help us to pray more earnestly, dear Father. In Jesus' name. Amen.

Jesus – Saviour and Lord

FOR READING & MEDITATION – ACTS 16:16–40

*'Believe in the Lord Jesus, and you will be saved –
you and your household.' (v31)*

We return now to the theme of Christ's lordship. When the slave girl who followed Paul and Silas was delivered from an evil spirit – a spirit of clairvoyance – it immediately affected the pockets of her owners. They had used her to make money for themselves by fortune-telling, and when the evil spirit had gone, their profits plummeted. In their anger they brought Paul and Silas before the magistrates, who ordered them to be beaten and thrown into prison.

Paul and Silas were probably unable to sleep because of the painful welts on their back, but remarkably they sing hymns of praise to God. Suddenly an earthquake shakes the prison, the doors swing open and everyone's chains are loosed. The jailer, awakened by the shock, sees the prison doors open and, thinking everyone has fled, is deeply disturbed. Since their security was the guarantee of his life, he decides to kill himself. But Paul cries out, 'Don't harm yourself! We are all here!' (v28). When the jailer sees that the prisoners have not fled, he asks Paul, 'What must I do to be saved?' (v30). Paul replies, 'Believe in the Lord Jesus, and you will be saved – you and your household.'

FURTHER STUDY

Psa. 24:1–10;
Acts 10:36;
1 Cor. 8:5–6

1. What did Peter declare?

2. What did Paul say?

Look at Paul's words again: 'Believe in the Lord Jesus Christ.' In the days of Paul and the other apostles, new believers were introduced immediately to the truth of Christ's lordship. There was no suggestion, as we said three days ago, that they could accept Jesus as Saviour and then, at some point in the future, commit themselves to Him as Lord. The Early Church spoke with one voice when it gave converts this message: if you want to be saved then you recognise Jesus' lordship over the whole of your life. There is no other way of salvation.

Lord God, again I pray that You will help Your Church not to fudge this issue in an effort to make it easy for people to be saved. Let Your Spirit be at work, highlighting truth and helping us stay close to Scripture. In Jesus' name. Amen.

Biblical evangelism

FOR READING & MEDITATION – ACTS 28:17–31

'he preached the kingdom of God and taught about the Lord Jesus Christ.' (v31)

Today we continue reflecting on the thought that one of the great distinctives of the Early Church was the emphasis on the lordship of Jesus. It's always been a matter of great interest to me that the last four words of the final verse of Acts are these: 'the Lord Jesus Christ'. We should not be surprised, for the words provide a fitting conclusion to a book that has made so much of His lordship. There is only one Jesus Christ; He is our Lord and Saviour Jesus Christ. And response to Jesus is response to the totality of His Person – He is both Saviour and Lord.

In Romans 14:9 Paul writes, 'For this very reason, Christ died and returned to life so that he might be...' What? When I start to quote that verse to people and ask them to fill in the blank, do you know what most say? 'Saviour.' When I ask 'Why do you say that?' they reply, 'That is the reason why Christ died and returned to life... to be our Saviour.' But that is not what Paul said. Listen to his words: 'For this very reason, Christ died and returned to life so that he might be the *Lord* of both the dead and the living.'

It's a half truth when, in our enthusiasm to reach out to those around us, we present the gospel in a way that suggests the important thing is finding forgiveness for one's sin. The real issue, the greater issue, is committing oneself to the living Lord. Forgiveness of sins is necessary before one can live in harmony with Christ, but important though the forgiveness of sins is – and let no one minimise it – what is of even greater importance is the commitment to Christ as Lord. Evangelism that does not make this clear is not worthy of the name.

FURTHER STUDY

Isa. 9:6–7;
John 3:22–31;
Eph. 1:22

1. What did John declare of Jesus?

2. What had Isaiah prophesied?

Lord God, deliver us from any confusion on this matter. Show us that You cannot be our Saviour unless we are willing to acknowledge You as our Lord. And help us as Your Church to make this clear to everyone. In Jesus' name we pray. Amen.

Mutiny in the ranks?

FOR READING & MEDITATION – LUKE 6:43–49

'Why do you call me, "Lord, Lord," and do not do what I say?' (v46)

We started this section by asking the question raised by John Stott: 'What is the master key doctrine in the Scriptures?' The answer is this: the lordship of Christ. When we acknowledge that Jesus is not only Saviour but also Lord, then we have the integrating point for our faith and our behaviour. This is a truth which I believe needs to be stressed more clearly.

'But we do believe in the lordship of Christ,' I hear you say. 'Fine,' I answer, 'but are you willing to look at the words of our text and apply them to yourself – without hesitation and argument?' The Living Bible paraphrases Jesus' words like this: 'So why do you call me "Lord" when you won't obey me?' The issue of obedience to Christ as Lord is a challenge to us as today's Church. Let's ask: who is calling the final shots? Is it the Commander or the troops? The soldiers or the General? When we 'do our own thing' it creates confusion and distraction from our great commission (Matt. 28:18–20). For example, when people come up against a scriptural truth that they don't like or exposes their sinful lifestyle, they say: 'Some biblical principles are very difficult to follow these days. We try our best to live up to them, but it isn't possible to practise them all.' That is a self-dependent life, trying to make life work ourselves. It is not the God-dependent life we have been called to.

FURTHER STUDY

Matt. 7:24–29;
John 14:23;
Heb. 2:3

1. What was Jesus' conclusion at the end of the Sermon on the Mount?

2. What question did the writer of Hebrews ask?

If we say we believe Jesus Christ is Lord but do not rely on Him to enable us to do what He calls us to do, then we are merely paying Him lip service. Let me remind you of an often-used statement: if we do not crown Him Lord of all, we do not crown Him Lord at all.

Father, I don't want to live as a self-dependent member of Your Church. Yet that is what I am when I merely pay lip service to the truth of Your lordship. Help me put my words into action. In Jesus' name I ask it. Amen.

A sense of the numinous

FOR READING & MEDITATION – ACTS 4:32–36

'With great power the apostles continued to testify to the resurrection of the Lord Jesus' (v33)

Before we examine further distinctives of the Early Church, let's once again remind ourselves why we are exploring this line of study. It is because when we see clearly how God established the Church in the very beginning, what energised it, and what its vital elements were, then we are in a better position to build and develop and grow as the Church today. When we compare the Church today with the Church of the first century there are differences. Naturally there are great cultural differences between the Church of the New Testament and the Church of today (particularly in the West), but it is not the cultural differences we are seeking to identify – it is the spiritual ones.

FURTHER STUDY

Dan. 10:4–18; Rev. 1:9–20

1. What did the pre-incarnate Christ say to Daniel?

2. What did the glorified Christ say to John?

Another distinctive of the Early Church that made it such a spiritual force and power was this: it had a strong and pervading sense of the numinous. The word 'numinous' doesn't appear very much in evangelical writings, but it was a favourite word of men such as C.S. Lewis, George MacDonald and Rudolph Otto. My dictionary defines it as 'sensing the presence of divinity; awe-inspiring'. It is a word that conveys the holy fear we experience when we become aware of our creaturehood, and realise that we stand in the presence of a holy God.

When John the apostle, banished to the island of Patmos, caught a vision of the glorified Christ, he 'fell at his feet as though dead' (Rev. 1:17). When Daniel became conscious that he was in God's presence, he said, 'I had no strength left, my face turned deathly pale' (Dan. 10:8). There can be no real complete knowledge of God unless there is some sense of the numinous. The Early Church experienced it.

Gracious and loving Father, You made the Early Church the standard by which all future growth could be measured. Forgive us that we miss the mark, and reveal this day our next steps. Restore us we pray. In Jesus' name. Amen.

Two out of fellowship

FOR READING & MEDITATION – ACTS 5:1–11

'Great fear seized the whole church and all who heard about these events.' (v11)

Now we look at an incident which took place in the Early Church that, perhaps more than any other happening, contributed to a powerful sense of the numinous.

Prior to the incident with Ananias and his wife Sapphira, there had been large accessions to the Church – 3,000 on the day of Pentecost, hundreds more as a result of the healing of the crippled man at the Beautiful Gate of the Temple, as well as those being converted day by day. But the judgment that fell upon Ananias and Sapphira temporarily stopped the rush because it created in the whole community a deep sense of godly reverence and fear. Ananias and Sapphira produced a serious fracture in the *koinonia* because they thought more about themselves than they did about the fellowship. Their sin was not that they sold the land and kept back some of the money for themselves, but that they lied about the transaction and pretended they got a price for it which differed from the amount they actually received. They were quite free to give their money to the Church or keep it for themselves – but they were not free to lie. Their root sin was hypocrisy, and it swiftly brought upon them the judgment of God.

But why was the penalty so severe? Because God wanted to show His people that His *koinonia* was not to be taken lightly. However slow to come to judgment God would appear in later times, this first sin against the Body (the Church) could not go unrecognised. If you ever need to be reminded of what God really thinks about hypocrisy in His Church then turn to Acts 5.

FURTHER STUDY

Jer. 9:5; 17:1–9; Gal. 6:7

1. What was Jeremiah's conclusion concerning the human condition?

2. What solemn word did Paul bring to the Galatians?

My Father and my God, in these days when You seem slower to come to judgment than You used to be, help me see that Your abhorrence of sin, like Your nature, is the same 'yesterday, today and for ever'. Keep this truth ever before me. Amen.

Overcoming power

FOR READING & MEDITATION – ACTS 19:8–20

'they were all seized with fear, and the name of the Lord Jesus was held in high honour.' (v17)

The incident we are looking at today not only increased the sense of the numinous in the believers but it had a profound effect upon the non-Christian community as well. The fame of Paul's ability to work miracles seems to have spread so widely that there was an attempt to imitate his power. Some itinerant exorcists undertook to pronounce the name of Jesus over those who had evil spirits. While the seven sons of Sceva (a Jewish priest) were doing this, an evil spirit recognised that the exorcists were using the name of Christ without His authority. This evil spirit then caused the man possessed by him to jump on those attempting to perform the exorcism and beat them.

To understand this unusual event we have to understand Ephesus. It was the seat of magic, of exorcism, and of belief in the powers of darkness. Paul worked extraordinary miracles there in order to demonstrate that the Jesus he proclaimed was greater than the prince of the powers of darkness. Against this background, Paul's letter to the Ephesians takes on a new perspective. (Look, for example, at Ephesians 1:19–23; 3:20; 5:11–12; 6:11–12.)

As a result of what happened to the sons of Sceva, who used Jesus' name without His authority, the whole community was seized with fear, and a great spiritual move took place. Believers confessed their former, and apparently their continued, performance of magical practices. The evidence that God's power was at work in the Early Church, overcoming every power set against Him, clearly contributed to a sense of the numinous. How we need that same power to be at work in our churches today.

FURTHER STUDY

Gen. 35:5;
Josh. 2:1–13;
2 Chron.
17:9–11

1. What did Rahab say to the spies?

2. What happened when the Book of the Law of the Lord was taught?

Lord God, help us, Your community, to live as You originally intended. We have come too far to turn back now. Remain with us, dear Lord, so that we see Pentecostal days again. Amen.

A developing trend

FOR READING & MEDITATION – ACTS 17:16–34

'he himself gives all men life and breath and everything else.' (v25)

We continue reflecting on the truth that the Early Church lived with a deep sense of the numinous. The first Christians were in awe of God and experienced His continuous holy presence. When we lose a sense of reverence for God it will not be long before we find ourselves rationalising our relationship, adapting His words to suit ourselves, and cauterising our consciences.

I have written before of my concern about the way in which God is often trivialised, packaged for entertainment, seen as a formula for success, or treated like a celestial slot machine. Some years ago, when in the United States on a speaking engagement, I watched a singing group perform. I say 'perform' because they hindered any opportunity to sing along with them by telling the congregation, 'We'll do the singing, you do the worship.' Like me, no doubt most in the congregation wanted to sing as we worshipped. Later the song leader said, 'Close your eyes now while I talk to the man upstairs and ask Him to bless you.' I shuddered as he said that and thought to myself: how impoverished all this is, how trite when compared to the experiences of the men and women of Scripture, especially those in the Early Church.

There is, I know, a fine line between being God's friend and being too much in awe of Him, but we need to be careful that over familiarity does not minimise the reality of God. It saddens and distresses me when God is referred to in 'chummy' ways. Personally, I do not know how it is possible to talk meaningfully about a God before whose glory we have not first trembled.

FURTHER STUDY

Exod. 15:11;
1 Sam. 6:20;
Isa. 6:1–13

1. What element of God's character is underlined?

2. What three elements of God's character did the seraphs focus on?

God, help me always to be in awe of You. Your own Son knew You better than anyone, yet called You 'Holy Father'. May this same sense of awe and reverence pervade my relationship with You too. In Jesus' name. Amen.

The way to worship

FOR READING & MEDITATION – HEBREWS 12:14–29

*'worship God acceptably with reverence and awe, for our
"God is a consuming fire."' (v28–29)*

How deep or widespread is the sense of the numinous in today's Church? In an age when God is viewed as someone who is becoming therapeutic rather than transcendent, not only by those who might be described as liberals, but by many evangelicals also, I fear we are making God too small. From the pulpits of traditional churches, and the unplanned pulpits of house groups, the Church is being subjected to references to God that reduce Him.

I am not arguing that we should lose the sense of familiarity that flows from the relationship we have as a son or daughter with our loving Father (God forbid!). However, we must be careful we do not allow that to lead us to an overfamiliarity which causes us to lose the sense of the numinous. Christians will always pay a price when they become overfamiliar with God. A right balance must be maintained. We draw near to a Heart that is filled with indescribable love, and yet as we draw near we are in awe. But why should we be afraid of someone we love? Doesn't the Bible tell us, 'There is no fear in love,' and that 'perfect love drives out fear' (1 John 4:18)? Yes, it does, but it is talking about a kind of fear that is different to the one I have been describing over these past few days. The fear I am talking about is a godly fear – a healthy reverence and respect for the authority and power of the almighty.

FURTHER STUDY

Job 28:28;
Prov. 1:1–7;
Rev. 15:4

1. What is the beginning of wisdom?

2. What did the victorious sing?

Is it not a tragedy that for all our biblical understanding, and all our claims about our experience of the Spirit's power, in our churches we still present a God who is small enough to fit inside our tiny brains? To truly know God we must learn to know Him as He really is, and not conjure up our own caricatures.

Lord God, help us achieve the right balance, so that we draw close to You in love yet maintain a respect and an awe for You that recognises how awesome You really are. In Jesus' name we pray. Amen.

The greatest of all rooms

FOR READING & MEDITATION – ACTS 2:1

'When the day of Pentecost came, they were all together in one place.' (v1)

Today we pause in our meditations on the distinctives of the Early Church to celebrate Pentecost Sunday. The disciples' experience at Pentecost was the catalyst for all that followed in the Acts of the Apostles and throughout history down to this very day.

An article appeared in an American magazine some time ago, which had these words as its title: 'Little rooms where new worlds were made'. It talked about some of the great rooms of history and the new worlds created from them.

FURTHER STUDY

1 Chron. 21:26;
2 Chron. 5:12–14;
Mal. 3:1–4

1. What is the link between prayer, praise, offerings and God's fire?

2. What did the fire do and how might that relate to us?

There was the chamber in Philadelphia where the Declaration of Independence was signed. There was also the room in London where Karl Marx wrote his communist classic *Das Kapital*. Then there was the room in the English seaside town of St Leonards on Sea where John Logie Baird succeeded in producing television. The article spoke of many other rooms, but by far the greatest of all rooms was that in which 120 disciples of Christ met in the days leading up to the day of Pentecost (see Acts 1:13). From that room came the beginnings of a new society – the Church. This is the only society which is of any ultimate consequence.

Let me encourage you on this Pentecost Sunday to open your heart to all that God has for you. Has the fire in your heart died down? Are you just coasting in your Christian life rather than walking side by side with Jesus through every hour of every day? Are you conscious that your spiritual life is becoming mundane? Then confess your fears and desires to God right now and ask Him to touch your life once again and set your heart on fire. Pray this prayer with me:

God, on this Pentecost Sunday breathe Your fire once again into my life. I confess my fears and desires and ask that You will touch me afresh. Holy Spirit, come and fill me to overflowing. In Christ's precious name I ask it. Amen.

Dangerous criticism

FOR READING & MEDITATION – ACTS 6:1–7

*'the Grecian Jews... complained against the Hebraic Jews because
their widows were being overlooked' (v1)*

Another distinctive of the Early Church was this: the ability to reconcile or hold together in unbroken fellowship strong people who differed. The passage before us today informs us that as the Early Church increased in numbers, the Grecian Jews began to complain that their widows were being overlooked in the daily distribution of food. The Living Bible puts it like this: 'But with the believers multiplying rapidly, there were rumblings of discontent.' The Greek word for 'rumblings' is *gongusmos*, meaning 'a complaint expressed in subdued tones'. In other words, murmuring and grumbling.

Now there is nothing wrong with criticism, providing it is presented openly and honestly. Criticism is dangerous, however, when it is expressed in murmurings and not brought out into the open. Fellowship is based on confidence and trust; unaddressed grumbling breaks that confidence. Once the apostles heard what was happening, they took immediate action to resolve the issue. Though they were novices in the art of church management, they knew, nevertheless, that matters such as injustice, inequality and dissension needed to be addressed directly and not simply prayed about.

FURTHER STUDY

Prov. 10:12;
15:18; 16:28;
28:25; 29:22;
Matt. 18:15–20

1. What sort of person stirs up dissension?

2. What principles did Jesus lay down?

How different matters would be today if the causes of dissension were faced and dealt with instead of being swept under the carpet in an atmosphere of superspirituality. The apostles acted promptly and resolved the situation. Churches have been split because the leaders decided to pray and not to act. It's not that prayer is unimportant; it's that some things need action. Nothing can be allowed to mar the unity of the Body. Nothing.

Father, please give the leaders of Your Church the courage and confidence they need to face and deal with every issue that threatens the unity of Your Body. In Christ's name I pray. Amen.

Building 'God's New Socie

27–29 September 2019

'GOD's there, listening for all who pray,
for all who pray and mean it.'
(Psalm 145:18, *The Message*)

With so many prayer events happening this year, it's so exciting to see the Church coming together in prayer in the UK and all over the world. A huge part of CWR's ministry has always been to encourage us to put our faith in action and continue the legacy of CWR founder Selwyn Hughes – to pray for a revival, and for God's love to sweep through the nation and pour out His presence on the communities in which we live – and one of the ways you can do that is by hosting your very own National Prayer Weekend event.

How you can get involved

Prayer needn't be complicated, and the National Prayer Weekend is a way for anyone and everyone, even people who've never tried praying before, to come together as a community and pray. The idea behind the weekend is simply this: reach out to your local community by inviting prayer requests from your friends, neighbours, local school, local doctors' surgery... think as globally as you like! Then, using the free online resources available,

n your neighbourhood!

set up your own NPW event – whether in your own living room for a couple of hours, or by getting your entire church together and praying solidly in shifts throughout the entire weekend. Pray for the requests you've received and see how God works where you live.

Many people are looking for answers, comfort and hope. You might find you're surprised at just how open many people are when it comes to prayer! Here's some feedback from last year's National Prayer Weekend:

'During the previous week, some of us had gone into the shops to ask shopkeepers if they had any prayer requests for us to pray through at our prayer evening. We ended up with a long list! At 11am, several of us went into the high street of our town and offered prayer for people who were out and about. As our town is fairly small, it was really easy to pray with people as we all know each other whether believers or not. We found folk receptive and grateful to receive prayer because we are in relationship with each other and not strangers.'
(Feedback from a NPW event in Buckinghamshire, 2018)

If you want to get involve with this year's National Prayer Weekend, you can access lots of free resources and other materials available to purchase by visiting **national-prayer-weekend.com**

Don't forget to sign up and add your pin to the map!

No place for prejudice

FOR READING & MEDITATION – ACTS 11:1–18

'they... praised God, saying, "So then, God has granted even the Gentiles repentance unto life."' (v18)

At present we are examining the ability of the Early Church to reconcile, or hold together in unbroken fellowship, strong people who differed. Today's passage shows us that the news of Peter's visit to the house of Cornelius reached Jerusalem before he did. This allowed the 'circumcision party' – the group who believed salvation was for Jews only – a little time to marshal their forces for an attack on Peter. When they met with him they asked quite directly, 'Why did you go to uncircumcised men and eat with them?' (v3, RSV). Peter replied by recounting the events we looked at earlier. The very fact that Luke repeats so much of what took place in Peter's own words is an indication that he regarded the incident as being of great importance. Peter recounted first the vision he received and the divine command to 'have no hesitation about going' (v12). Then he told how, as he was speaking, the Holy Spirit fell on everyone in Cornelius' house 'as he had come on us at the beginning' (v15). As they listened to Peter, they could not help but be moved, and concluded with him that 'God has granted even the Gentiles repentance unto life'.

FURTHER STUDY

Lev. 19:15;
Job 13:10;
1 Tim. 5:21;
James 2:1–13

1. What did Paul urge Timothy to do?

2. What was James' indictment?

It wasn't easy for Peter to go to the home of Cornelius, a Gentile, and it wasn't easy for the Jewish Christians to admit Gentiles. The fact that they did is a tremendous testimony to their openness and responsiveness to the work of the Holy Spirit, who was moving in their midst. Any personal prejudice at this critical moment in the life of the Early Church could have brought it to a halt. How wonderful it would be if prejudice or preconceptions were dealt with as easily in the modern-day Church as they were in this.

Our Father, give us such an experience of the Holy Spirit, and such a love for Christ, that we, in the Church of today, will have the ability the Early Church had to hold together strong people who differ. In Christ's name we ask it. Amen.

'You need grace!'

FOR READING & MEDITATION – ACTS 15:36–41

'They had such a sharp disagreement that they parted company.'
(v39)

After Paul and Barnabas had returned to Antioch from their missionary tour of Asia, Paul wanted to visit the churches again. Barnabas agreed, but was eager to take John Mark with them. But Paul resisted this, and a paraphrase of his remarks might read: 'John Mark let us down when he deserted us on our missionary tour. We can't afford to take someone unreliable. Let's forget him.'

After a while the disagreement got more heated, and the two men became so irritated with one another that they decided to part company. *The Message* paraphrases today's verse like this: 'Tempers flared, and they ended up going their separate ways.' This split could easily have led to the start of two denominations – the Paulites, who believed the Church should be for fully committed and reliable believers, and the Barnabites, who believed people should be given another chance. Holders of both views might well have felt justified in starting a different denomination, but thankfully this did not happen. Who was right and who was wrong? In my opinion, Paul was right in saying that John Mark ought not to have left them, but perhaps wrong in not giving him a second chance.

The church at Antioch was well aware of the strong differences between the two men and was no doubt deeply concerned for them. It's interesting that when Paul and Silas – the man Paul chose to replace Barnabas – departed on their journey, they were 'commended by the brothers to the grace of the Lord' (v40). I wonder if they did it with a twinkle in their eye and said inwardly, 'Paul and Silas, you need it!' For it's only grace that can keep strong men pulling together.

FURTHER STUDY

Col. 4:1–10;
2 Tim. 4:9–11;
Philem. 23–24

1. What is clear about Paul's relationship to John Mark?

2. Is there anyone to whom you need to be reconciled?

Father, even now, as I pray, somewhere in Your Church strong spiritual men and women will be differing – and may even be in danger of parting company. Let Your grace flow in and prevail, I pray. In Jesus' name. Amen.

'A grand Christian'

FOR READING & MEDITATION – 2 TIMOTHY 4:1–18

'Get Mark and bring him with you, because he is helpful to me in my ministry.' (v11)

We continue reflecting on the sharp division that arose between Barnabas and Paul. Luke, as we saw yesterday, honestly reported the scenario: 'They had such a sharp disagreement that they parted company,' he said (Acts 15:39). *Paroxusmos*, or 'paroxysm', is the word Luke actually used, and although in his day it may not have conveyed such violent emotion as it does today, the word still indicates that there was an angry dispute.

But sharp though the disagreement was, good came out of it. If Paul and Barnabas had travelled together, they would have gone to Cyprus and Galatia. One commentator explains that this would have consumed all their energy. However, by going separately, Paul finished his visitation of the churches in Galatia with enough strength left to look for new worlds to win for Christ.

FURTHER STUDY

1 Cor. 9:6; Gal. 2:1–10

1. What is clear from Paul's account of events at Jerusalem?

2. Besides himself, who is Paul arguing the case for?

Another point to be noted is that John Mark was reclaimed for the work of Christ, and there is little doubt that Barnabas had much to do with it. One writer suggests that when Paul sat down in later years to write the words in today's text, the scribe might have looked up with a quizzical smile as if to say, 'You really mean that? Mark, helpful in your ministry?' Whereupon Paul possibly replied, 'Yes, he is – and Barnabas had much to do with that. Barnabas was a better man than me. He was always taking up with people who others might find difficult to associate with. He pleaded my cause when nobody believed in me. A great man, Barnabas.' Perhaps a tear then trickled down his cheek. Whatever had gone wrong in the past, it was now forgiven and forgotten.

Father, how good it is when sharp divisions between Christians are forgiven and forgotten. Reconciliation has the marks of the cross upon it – marks of love and restoration. Please help me restore any broken relationships. Amen.

Disagreeing agreeably

FOR READING & MEDITATION – 2 CORINTHIANS 5:11–21

'*God... has committed to us the message of reconciliation.*' (v19)

For one more day we consider the need for reconciliation between strong personalities who differ sharply with one another. Before I became a Christian I had the idea that there were no disputes between Christians in the first century; such things, I thought, happened only among Christians of today. After I became a Christian I began to make a special study of the Acts of the Apostles, and at once I saw that the men and women of the first century were exactly the same kind of people as we are. If the Early Church had not been so taken up with Jesus, so filled with the Spirit, and so committed to reconciliation, it might not have survived.

Today's Church does not always appear to be as successful at reconciling differences as were the early Christians. Huge divisions split our churches. And the difficulty is not so much that Christians disagree – but that they disagree so disagreeably. It ought to be possible for those who are 'in Christ' to maintain a loving spirit even though they see things from different points of view.

I wrote that last sentence tongue-in-cheek for, as I look back, I am aware there have been times in my own life when I have failed in this respect. However, I don't think there has ever been an occasion when, after a short period of time, I have not sought reconciliation. Strong people will differ, and sometimes differ sharply, but the Church must always point them to the way of reconciliation. Any church that does not do that is not following the example set by the Church of the New Testament. Reconciliation is the heart of the gospel; all else is subsidiary.

FURTHER STUDY

John 13:34–35;
Rom. 5:1–10;
2 Cor. 5:18–20;
Col. 1:22

1. What is the heart of the gospel message?

2. How can we demonstrate this to a broken world?

Lord God, please bring Your Church to the place where it is a redeeming and a reconciling community. For how can we preach reconciliation to a lost world when we ourselves remain unreconciled? Help us, dear Father. In Jesus' name. Amen.

The first Christian martyr

FOR READING & MEDITATION – ACTS 7:51–60

*'While they were stoning him, Stephen prayed,
"Lord Jesus, receive my spirit."' (v59)*

A further distinctive of the Early Church was this: there was no distinction between what we refer to as laity and clergy. Although Luke's book is called 'The Acts of the Apostles', it records some significant things which were done by people who were not apostles – such as the man we have read about today. We looked at Stephen earlier, but now we examine his life from a different perspective.

Stephen was one of those who were chosen to 'wait on tables' (6:2). He was a man of the ranks – a layman. We are told he was 'full of faith and of the Holy Spirit' (6:5), and 'full of God's grace and power' (6:8). People with these characteristics can often stir up strong reactions in others, although it does not usually produce the kind of consequence that fell upon Stephen. Some members of the synagogue tried to debate with Stephen, but his wisdom and knowledge of Scripture was too much for them (6:9–10). So, feeling grieved that they had lost the debate, they embarked upon a course of deceit and cunning that led to him becoming the first Christian martyr.

Stephen lost his life under a shower of stones. Did the godless win? Apparently, but only apparently, for look at the sequel. Standing in the crowd, 'holding the coats', was Saul of Tarsus. I don't think he ever forgot Stephen's prayer as the stones pounded the life out of him. I have no doubt that occasion was one of many events that led to his conversion. The stones are still there somewhere, now trodden underfoot, but the Spirit of Christ which was in Stephen marches deathless through the ages. Stone it and you simply scatter it throughout the earth.

FURTHER STUDY

Acts 6:3–15;
8:2; 11:19;
22:20–21

1. How did the group describe Stephen and respond to his death?

2. What was the result of the persecution of Stephen?

Father, drive deep within me the truth that Your truth, will and purposes always prevail. In You I have hold of something that nothing can hold back. And for that I am eternally grateful. Amen.

'Philip the Evangelist'

FOR READING & MEDITATION – ACTS 8:4–13,26–40

*'Philip went down to a city in Samaria and proclaimed the
Christ there.' (v5)*

Today we think about another significant member of the
laity – Philip. He too was one of 'the Seven' chosen to
'wait on tables' (6:3–4). But the reach of Philip's ministry went
beyond the reach of his hand; he wanted to distribute the
gospel as well as distribute goods. Philip was a man whose
evangelistic gifting went beyond his role. He is an inspiration
to all those ordinary men and women who want to serve Jesus.

Philip went down to a city in Samaria and preached Christ
to crowds of people there – and many became Christians
as a result. Soon the Jerusalem Church sent Peter
and John to lay hands on the converts so they
might receive the Holy Spirit. The Samaritans, you
remember, were the people who would not receive
Jesus 'because his face was set toward Jerusalem'
(Luke 9:53, RSV). Two disciples had wanted to call
fire down from heaven on them (Luke 9:54). Now
two apostles were calling down upon them, not the
fire of judgment but the fire of the Spirit!

Right in the middle of this amazing mission, Philip
is sent to meet someone in the desert. Fancy being
sent into a desert! Yet Philip doesn't hesitate to follow
this guidance and move from a place where he was
ministering to thousands to a congregation of one – the
Ethiopian eunuch.

Philip was not a theologian like Peter or Paul, but he knew
enough about the gospel to lead a soul to Christ. To have a firm
hold on the basic truths of the gospel, and to feel responsibility
for sharing it with others, is to stand in the splendid tradition
of this great layman who, over the years, has earned the
distinction of being known as 'Philip the Evangelist'.

FURTHER STUDY

John 1:43–50;
12:20–22;
Acts 21:8–9

1. Who did Philip the apostle bring to Christ?

2. What is said of Philip the Evangelist's household?

**Lord, this is indeed the greatest work in the world – introducing
others to You. No matter what my role in life, help me to see that
You can use me to share Jesus. Someone shared Him with me; may
I be used to share Him with others. Amen.**

'Son of Encouragement'

FOR READING & MEDITATION – ACTS 9:19–31

'When he came to Jerusalem, he tried to join the disciples, but they were all afraid of him' (v26)

Another great layman who comes to prominence in the book of Acts is Barnabas – a man on whom we have already focused a little. He pops up in so many different places in the book that we have to move around to get a full portrait of him.

The first appearance of Barnabas is in Acts 4:36–37, where we see him selling his land and bringing the money to lay at the apostles' feet. He appears next in 9:26–27, where we observe him befriending Saul of Tarsus and introducing him to the apostles in Jerusalem. Then, in 11:25–26, we see

FURTHER STUDY

1 Thess. 4:18;
Heb. 3:12–13;
10:25

1. What are we to do daily?
2. Is there someone you can be a Barnabas to today?

him seeking out Paul to be his co-worker. He is described as 'a good man, full of the Holy Spirit and faith' (11:24). Barnabas, whose name means 'Son of Encouragement' (4:36), was a man who had a large heart and a magnanimous spirit, especially where people in need of help were concerned.

Today's passage brings out this point most sharply. Saul of Tarsus came down from Damascus to Jerusalem to share his testimony with the apostles, but we read, 'they were all afraid of him, not believing that he really was a disciple' (v26). Look, though, at the next verse: 'But Barnabas took him and brought him to the apostles. He told them how Saul on his journey had seen the Lord'. Here, in the presence of the sceptical disciples, Barnabas demonstrated that he was a person who would not hold a new convert at arm's length and would not doubt his conversion because of the great harm that he had previously done the Church.

Barnabas welcomed a man who needed acceptance and couldn't get it. It's sad when Christian disciples are so orthodox in their theology but so hardened in their sympathy.

Father, help me never to be like that – keep me orthodox in my theology and tender-hearted I pray. May I, by accepting Your forgiveness, mirror Your forgiveness. In Jesus' name. Amen.

A place for everyone

FOR READING & MEDITATION – 1 CORINTHIANS 12:12–31

'Now you are the body of Christ, and each one of you is a part of it.'
(v27)

Over the past few days we have looked at three laymen whose ministry in some ways matched that of the apostles. They show us that Jesus, the Head of the Church, has a purpose for every one of us in His Body.

During the Reformation, set in motion by Martin Luther, the principle of the priesthood of all believers was taught. However, it's a pity that the Reformers failed to make it even more clear that the laity (as they are referred to) are as truly and as fully the servants of Christ in the Church, and as responsible for its functioning, as those who have been ordained. A phrase which encapsulates this is: 'the apostolate of the laity'. The word 'laity' comes from the Greek word *laos*, and simply means 'people'. 'Apostle' comes from a word that means 'sent'. The Church here in the twenty-first century needs to take note that when Jesus said to the disciples, 'As the Father has sent me, I am sending you [or apostling you]' (John 20:21), He was commissioning the whole Church.

A papal encyclical issued by Pope Pius X in 1906, entitled *Vehementer Nos*, said, 'As for the masses, they have no other right than that of letting themselves be led and of following their pastors as a docile flock.' That, of course, is a view with which many Catholic theologians disagree today, but there are still people in some sections of the Church who think that the ministers who operate from the front of the church are the only ones who should do the work of Christ. Once, while ministering in Malaysia, the church notice sheet had on it these words: 'Ministers – the entire congregation.' I smiled to myself as I thought, 'You've got it.'

FURTHER STUDY

Rom. 12:1–8;
Eph. 1:23;
Col. 1:24; 2:19

1. What does Paul teach the Romans?

2. How is the Church described?

Father, help me find my place in Your Body, for I see that if I don't then I am like a square peg in a round hole. Show me, Lord, just what You want me to do, and where You want me to be. In Christ's name I pray. Amen.

Church growth

FOR READING & MEDITATION – ACTS 4:1–12

'But many who heard the message believed, and the number of men grew to about five thousand.' (v4)

Now we come to the penultimate section of our meditations on the distinctives of the Early Church. The theme we are going to focus on over the next few days is this: the first Church was a growing Church to which converts were added in ever increasing numbers.

The first influx of people took place on the day of Pentecost when Peter, using the keys of the kingdom of heaven previously promised to him by Christ (Matt. 16:19), opened up the doors of the Church – and 3,000 souls streamed in (2:41). Add to that the 120 who had already started to follow Christ before Pentecost (1:15), and the many hundreds to whom He appeared in the days following the resurrection (on one occasion He appeared to 500 of His disciples at once – see 1 Cor. 15:6). There must have been at least 4,000 of Jesus' followers now in and around Jerusalem in the first few days after Pentecost. From then on, souls were added to the Church daily (2:47). As someone has put it: 'He did not save them without adding them to the Church, and He did not add them to the Church without saving them.'

FURTHER STUDY

Hosea 2:23;
Mark 4:30–34;
Acts 13:48;
Eph. 3:6

1. To what did Jesus liken the kingdom of God?

2. What had Hosea prophesied?

Then, following the miracle performed on the crippled man at the Beautiful Gate of the Temple (3:1–9), we read today that the number of men grew to 5,000. Please notice that the figure given here is only for the men, and we can assume that about the same number of women also became committed followers of the Christ. In Acts 5:14 and 6:7 still more growth is recorded. Some Church historians reckon that just four weeks after Pentecost there must have been around 12,000 to 15,000 converts in the Early Church. Now that's Church growth! And there was more to follow.

Father, as I reflect on the wave after wave of new believers who streamed into the Early Church, and how today in some churches we do not see much growth from one year to another, my heart cries out: do it again, dear Lord, do it again. Amen.

God has no energy crisis

FOR READING & MEDITATION – ACTS 4:23–30

'Stretch out your hand to heal and perform miraculous signs and wonders' (v30)

Yesterday we saw how in the first few weeks after Pentecost the Church grew from 120 to approximately 12,000 to 15,000 people. This brings us to an intriguing question: what particular method did the Church employ in order to bring people to a place of faith and trust in the recently crucified Jesus? It might be helpful if we looked a little at how the Early Church grew, and what caused its phenomenal expansion.

First, the Jerusalem Church reached the size it did because of the empowering ministry of the Holy Spirit and miracles. There were, for example, the amazing events at Pentecost – people speaking in languages they had never learned. It is true that it was Peter's clear message that finally convinced the crowd, but it was the miracles that first got their attention. Notice also that supernatural things did not stop happening after Pentecost. The post-Pentecost period is filled with accounts of wonderful events, such as outstanding healings (some were even healed when standing in Peter's shadow, 5:15), a building being shaken by the power of God (4:31), prison doors opening of their own(!) accord (5:19; 12:10), two people being struck down dead because of their deception (5:1–10), and so on.

FURTHER STUDY

John 3:1–2; 10:34–42; Acts 8:1–8

1. What did Nicodemus declare?

2. Why did the crowds pay close attention to what Philip said?

There can be little doubt that the Holy Spirit in the Early Church had a tremendous pulling power on the hearts of the people. But can we expect similar manifestations today? It must be acknowledged that different convictions are held within the Church about these things, but I believe we can. God doesn't have an energy crisis. His Spirit still works in great power in some parts of the world today. Why not where we are?

Yes Father – why not? Can it be that we are more problem-conscious than power-conscious? Although we do not hanker after miracles alone, surely they are still part of Your purposes. Visit us today, dear Lord. In Jesus' name. Amen.

No place for the spurious

FOR READING & MEDITATION – JOHN 14:1–15

*'anyone who has faith in me will do what I have been doing.
He will do even greater things than these' (v12)*

The matter of the miraculous is such a contentious issue in the Church all around the world that we spend another day considering it. Because so-called 'healing evangelists' circulate within the Church, we should discern and consider the miraculous and ask: can we really expect miracles and supernatural events to take place today in the way they did in the Early Church? Wasn't the miraculous merely an element that was necessary to get the Church going, but now it is established, aren't we supposed to be walking by faith?

FURTHER STUDY

Acts 3:1–16;
5:16; 9:34;
14:8–18

1. How did Peter and John react to the crowd's response?

2. How did Paul and Barnabas react to the crowd's response?

The idea that God withdrew the supernatural and the miraculous from the Church a few decades after Pentecost, I believe, is scripturally untenable. Dr Martyn Lloyd-Jones, in true expository manner, has laid that idea to rest in a number of his books. It is my personal belief that God intends the supernatural and the miraculous to be as much part of today's Church as it was of the Early Church.

However, having said that, I must add that I deplore the fact that where there is no evidence of the supernatural and the truly miraculous, people try to create it by psychological means. A number (not all) of the healings seen in today's large healing meetings are, in my opinion, psychologically induced. In the New Testament it wasn't the apostles or evangelists who made a fuss about healing, but the people who were healed! Think, for instance, of the lame man at the Beautiful Gate (3:8–10). I have longed to see the miraculous power of God at work in His Church today – just as it was in Bible days, but I loathe what is spurious. And perhaps it's the spurious that is stopping the reality coming through.

Lord God, if it is the spurious that is holding back the pure stream of Your Spirit then flush it out we pray. Give us once again the pure stream of Pentecost – the power that nothing can gainsay. In Jesus' name we ask it. Amen.

The peril of second best

FOR READING & MEDITATION – ACTS 6:1–7

'So the word of God spread... and a large number of priests became obedient to the faith.' (v7)

A second factor that contributed to the amazing growth of the Early Church was the release of the apostles for the work of the ministry. Consider this issue carefully with me, for there is more to it than at first appears.

When 'the Seven' had taken over the administrative tasks, the apostles had the opportunity to concentrate entirely on doing what they did best – teaching and preaching. There can be little doubt that transferring the administrative tasks to 'the Seven' marked a turning point in the life of that first Christian community. It is interesting that once this was done we read 'a large number of priests became obedient to the faith'. We can only assume that this was a direct result of the apostles being able to focus entirely on prayer and the work of making known the truths concerning Christ and the Church. The apostles were led by the Spirit to differentiate between the good and the best. What they were doing in administration was good, but it was not the best. The best was to give themselves to God in prayer and concentrate on presenting the Word in a clear and effective way.

FURTHER STUDY

Luke 10:38–42;
2 Tim. 2:1–7

1. What did Jesus say of Mary?

2. What did Paul say to Timothy about civilian affairs?

One of the devil's favourite devices is to get the Church engaged in doing things that are second best, thus robbing them of their real cutting edge. How many modern churches, I wonder, have fallen into the trap of expecting their spiritual leaders to be estate agents, transport managers, financial advisers, and so on, rather than ministers of the Word? The present-day Church, like the Church of the first century, needs to realise the importance of the division of labour so that people can fulfil their God-given roles and avoid the peril of second best.

Lord God, how desperately we need the wisdom of the Spirit, for sometimes it is very difficult to differentiate between the good and the best. Baptise us afresh with heavenly wisdom that we might see – really see. In Jesus' name. Amen.

A domestic context

'Day after day... they never stopped teaching and proclaiming the good news' (v42)

Another factor that contributed to the phenomenal growth of the Early Church was the way in which the disciples shared with each other in small groups. In addition to meeting together as a large congregation in Solomon's Colonnade, they continued that fellowship in smaller groups in their homes. Listen to the way in which the Amplified Bible words Acts 2:46: 'And day after day they regularly assembled in the temple with united purpose, and in their homes they broke bread [including the Lord's Supper].' They supplemented the large services with more informal gatherings in their homes.

FURTHER STUDY

Matt. 9:10;
Mark 14:3;
Luke 10:38;
19:7;
John 12:1–8

1. Which home did Jesus often visit?

2. How often do you share Jesus with someone in your home?

Even though the Scriptures do not say so precisely, I think it highly likely that many came to faith in people's homes. Today's text tells us that from house to house the teaching concerning the crucified and resurrected Jesus continued and was a constant theme. Nothing held back the apostles from teaching and sharing, both in the Temple and in the people's homes. But this was not the only form of Christian witness. As friends and families went in and out of the homes where believers were present, I feel sure they would have been drawn to the Christian faith by what they observed.

Vital as it is for the health of a local church to meet together corporately, it is also valuable to meet in smaller more informal gatherings. Those who practice this, and invite along those who are not yet Christians, say that people are often more ready to receive Christ in a home than in a formal church setting. Amazing ministry can come out of a home where Christ is the head, and where the doors are open to those who do not yet know Him.

My Father and my God, I know You are as much at home in a cottage as You are in a church, for You see Your Church not as a brick building but as a living Body. Help me to see it in the same way. In Jesus' name I pray. Amen.

Next Issue

JUL/AUG 2019

Under the Sun

Many of us strive to find a sense of purpose for our lives in our work, relationships, wealth, knowledge or recreation, but with limited success. Ultimately, what is the meaning of life on this earth?

In the book of Ecclesiastes, Solomon asks the timeless questions that are still asked by today's world. Next issue, join us as we journey through some of these questions and discover that it is only when we understand life under the sun in the context of God's eternal purposes that our lives find purpose, fulfilment, and true hope for the future.

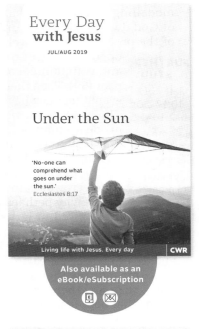

Also available as an eBook/eSubscription

Obtain your copy from CWR, a Christian bookshop or your National Distributor.
If you would like to take out a subscription, see the order form at the back of these notes.

Original-style evangelism

FOR READING & MEDITATION – ACTS 8:1–8

'When the crowds heard Philip and saw the miraculous signs he did, they all paid close attention to what he said.' (v6)

The Early Church, we have been seeing, expanded in the way it did for three primary reasons: the presence of the Holy Spirit, the powerful teaching of the apostles, and the daily witness of the believers in their homes.

One of the main ministries of the Church in this early period was establishing those who became believers and modelling for all time what can happen when the people of God dwell together in unity. And this went on in spite of the problems the Church faced, which included strong opposition from the Jewish authorities (4:1; 5:17), and complaints concerning the treatment of the poor (6:1). Then there was the death of Stephen – an event that must have been a severe blow to the Early Church. But during the persecution that followed his death many of Jesus' followers were scattered throughout Judea and Samaria.

FURTHER STUDY

Matt. 5:12;
10:17–20;
2 Tim. 2:10–12

1. How are we to respond to persecution?

2. What did Paul promise Timothy?

Philip, one of those who served with Stephen (6:5), conducted mass evangelism in Samaria, during which crowds came to listen to what he said. Here we see why perhaps God allowed persecution to hit the Church in Jerusalem. It was not because the believers were failing to extend the Church there but because the message now needed to be heard 'in all Judea and Samaria, and to the ends of the earth' (1:8).

Psalm 133 says that when God's people live together in unity, then it is there the Lord imparts His blessing. And it seems that both history and experience have shown us that the most powerful and successful evangelistic efforts are those made by a church that knows true *koinonia* and real spiritual unity. That kind of evangelism rarely fails.

Father, help us understand that we cannot be evangelical without being evangelistic. And show us also that evangelism which is practised by a church in unity is evangelism according to Your pattern. In Jesus' name we pray. Amen.

Another King

FOR READING & MEDITATION – ACTS 5:25–32

'Peter and the other apostles replied: "We must obey God rather than men!"' (v29)

Now we come to the last on our list of the Early Church's distinctives: their unswerving allegiance to Christ and His eternal kingdom. The first Christians, while maintaining respect for the civil authorities that were over them, saw that their primary allegiance was to the laws and principles of the kingdom of God. They never planned or even thought to overthrow the ruling authorities, but sought only to live their lives in harmony with the truths being taught by the apostles.

The passage we have read today brings out this thought most clearly. The high priest and his associates ordered the arrest of the apostles and put them in jail, but during the night an angel of the Lord opened the doors of the jail and set them free. Before leaving them, however, the angel gave them a command that was contrary to the wishes of the high priest: 'Go, stand in the temple courts... and tell the people the full message of this new life' (v20).

An issue that puzzles many Christians is the matter of obedience to authority. They ponder such scriptures as Romans 13:1, where we are told that 'Everyone must submit himself to the governing authorities', and then consider today's passage where the apostles' actions differed to wishes of the spiritual authority of the high priest – and wonder how can these two forms of behaviour be reconciled. The answer is this: we are expected to live in obedience to earthly authorities unless they are contrary to God's design for living. The apostles were not out to overthrow the systems of their day; they simply understood that Jesus had first call on their lives and relationships.

FURTHER STUDY

Dan. 3:13–30;
John 18:28–36

1. What assertion did the Hebrew young men make?

2. What did Jesus reply to Pilate?

Our Father and our God, we come to You once again to ask that You will help us understand Your priorities. May we always remember that while we have a responsibility to be good citizens in this world, we live first for You. Amen.

A right response

FOR READING & MEDITATION – ACTS 23:1–11

'Paul replied, "Brothers, I did not realise that he was the high priest"'
(v5)

We continue considering the thought that the early believers, while respecting the authorities that were over them, gave themselves first to Jesus and His will. Some commentators claim that the Early Church, being 'God's new society', completely disregarded the old systems of authority and government. However, the passage before us highlights that viewpoint to be false.

When the apostle Paul was brought before the Sanhedrin, Ananias, the high priest, commanded those who were close to Paul to strike him on the mouth. Paul, understanding that the order implied he was a liar, reacted to this and, in condemning Ananias, called the high priest a 'whitewashed wall' (v3). When it was made clear to Paul that it was the high priest he was addressing, he immediately apologised, and brought himself under the authority of Scripture by saying, 'I did not realise that he was the high priest; for it is written: "Do not speak evil about the ruler of your people" [Exod. 22:28]' (v5). Paul was clearly offended by the command of the high priest, but when he discovered that he was talking to a man with spiritual authority, he knew that he should show respect.

FURTHER STUDY

Rom. 13:1–7;
1 Pet. 2:17

1. What do we do when we rebel against authority?

2. How does Paul describe rulers in authority?

But how could Paul respect a man who had just ordered him to be hit across the mouth? By focusing not so much on the person but on his position. When we respect the position of those over us in authority because we have a high regard for the principle of authority, then it helps to transform our view of the situation. It may not stop the person over us continuing to be difficult, but because of our biblical response it will make God's grace available to us.

Lord God, I see that a right response to authority is one of our supreme responsibilities. May we not be confused over this matter. Help us to respect those that You have given authority over us. For the sake of Your dear Son. Amen.

In tune with heaven

FOR READING & MEDITATION – ROMANS 12:1–8

'Do not conform any longer to the pattern of this world' (v2)

If there is one thing that is becoming clear as we examine this last distinctive of the Early Church, it is this: the believers of that day not only followed the laws and principles of the society in which they lived, but ultimately the principles and practices of God's kingdom.

The Church of the first century marched through the world to the beat of a different drum. I'd like to borrow the words of the American essayist, Thoreau, who said: 'If a man does not keep pace with his companions, perhaps it's because he hears a different drummer. Let him step to the music he hears, however measured or far away.' The beat the early Christians listened to came not from around, but from above. Their spiritual ears were tuned in to the music of heaven, and they tried to keep in step with that, even though it brought them into direct conflict with the world.

FURTHER STUDY

Eph. 4:17–24;
Phil. 3:15–20;
Col. 3:1–2

1. What did Paul point out to the Ephesians?

2. What did he exhort the Colossians to do?

Earlier we saw that following the death of Ananias and Sapphira, 'No-one else dared join them, even though they were highly regarded by the people' (5:13). Yet the next verse says, 'Nevertheless, more and more men and women believed in the Lord and were added to their number.' The two verses appear to be contradictory, but really they are not. The death of Ananias and Sapphira (as we saw) produced in the community a sense that the Church was a society in which a remarkable power and presence was at work. This produced a sense of awe in people that to become a Christian meant coming under the lordship of Christ, and involved personal cost because of belonging to a community that shared sacrificially with others. How different things would be if this were the case today.

Father, help Your Church today to march to the beat of heaven's music and not to be influenced by the ideas of the world. May we seek first the kingdom of God and let all other things become secondary. In Christ's name we ask it. Amen.

True non-conformity

FOR READING & MEDITATION – ACTS 8:18–24

'Peter answered: "May your money perish with you, because you thought you could buy the gift of God with money!"' (v20)

Yesterday we commented that if those who belonged to the Early Church did not keep in step with the rest of society it was because they marched to the beat of a different drum. Our challenge in the Church of today is to pick up that beat and make a determined choice to follow it.

In today's reading we find the apostle Peter turning down Simon's offer of money for the power to be able to lay hands on people and see them receive the Holy Spirit. Was Peter tempted to respond to Simon's offer of financial reward? I doubt it. This man, who at one time was like a reed blown in the wind, is now as steady as a rock. His only concern is to serve the interests of Jesus and His people.

FURTHER STUDY

Mark 8:27–30;
John 6:60–70

1. How did Peter respond to the question Jesus put?

2. What conclusion did he come to?

As I thought of Simon Peter, and others in the Early Church who stood out against the trends and ideas of their day because they marched to the beat of heaven's music, I called to mind the writer and broadcaster Malcolm Muggeridge who, in the latter years of his life, openly confessed to being a follower of Jesus. While he was rector of Edinburgh University, he discovered that the university authorities were giving out free contraceptives to students without permitting any pastoral support or Christian counsel in the area of premarital sex. Unable to support the university's decision, he resigned. His farewell address was widely reported. Malcolm Muggeridge concluded his speech from the pulpit of St Giles' Cathedral in Edinburgh with these powerful words: 'The reason why I resign from my duties today is because I cannot go along with this. I belong to another kingdom and to another King – one Jesus.'

Father God, if ever I am placed in a situation where I have to choose between Your ways and the ways of the world, may I have the courage to go Your way. In Jesus' name I pray. Amen.

Picking up the beat

'As obedient children, do not conform to the evil desires you had when you lived in ignorance.' (v14)

Having thought for the last two days about how the first-century Church marched to the beat of a different drum, we must now ask ourselves this searching question: who are we, the Church of the twenty-first century, in step with? The world around, or the world without end? Society today mostly disregards the Church, frequently see it as source of comedy, and few really understand its outworking and calling, and so live, they believe, as good a life as their church-attending neighbours. The Church is made up of individuals. And it's sad when we miss the greatest evangelistic impact highlighted for us by Jesus in John 13:34–35: 'Let me give you a new command: Love one another. In the same way I loved you, you love one another. This is how everyone will recognize that you are my disciples – when they see the love you have for each other' (*The Message*).

The Church in Acts was 'highly regarded by the people' (Acts 5:13); but can we claim that such high regard is paid to the Church from all sections of society today?

There is no doubt that today's Church is contributing and giving considerably to the wider community. However, I wonder, if we are really to be more like the Early Church and be effective in this generation, then we must stop trying to be like the world and rediscover the original design. The Church is not misunderstood by the world because it is like Jesus; it is misunderstood because it is not like Him. When we stop trying to keep in step with the music of the world and march to the beat of a different drum, we will make a far more powerful impression. Again I say: the greatest challenge of our time is to pick up heaven's beat – and follow it.

FURTHER STUDY

Psa. 51:10;
85:1–6;
Isa. 40:31

1. What was the psalmist's prayer?

2. Make it your prayer today.

Father, again we pray, help us – we who form today's Christian community – not to conform to the patterns of the world, but to march to the beat of heaven's drum. For that beat, we know, is the right beat. In Jesus' name we ask it. Amen.

The return

FOR READING & MEDITATION – JEREMIAH 6:9–20

'This is what the LORD says: "Stand at the crossroads and look;
ask for the ancient paths"' (v16)

O n this, the last day of these meditations in which we have been taking a look at the Church – 'God's new society' – what are our conclusions? The first is this: when we put the Church of today alongside the Church of the first century, we cannot help but see that there are major differences. Naturally, we must be balanced about this, for there are so many things for which we are thankful, but nevertheless the truth remains – we have not arrived, there is much to learn and much to live out in our daily lives together in our communities.

FURTHER STUDY

Josh. 24:14–24;
Matt. 12:30;
Mark 9:40;
Luke 16:13

1. What was the challenge of Joshua's day?

2. What is the challenge we face?

Second, as we think about the future and how we can live and apply the new truths we may have discovered, we also consider how we can return to the old paths – to the sincerity, eagerness and enthusiasm of those first-century Christians. When we see how the original Church practised everyday life, we can more easily spot the differences. There are cultural variances between now and then of course, but we cannot use the cultural differences as an excuse for failing to see the spiritual differences.

Third, although challenging, it's important to go often to the book of Acts and take whatever steps are necessary to make our fellowships a living illustration of what community life in Jesus is like. In every hamlet, village, town and city the local church needs to ask itself: are we reflecting to the world around us that we are citizens of heaven? If we fail to do this, says one commentator, then it may well be that in the twenty-first century the Church could be 'a conscious minority surrounded by an arrogant militant paganism'. Let's give ourselves afresh to God, and make sure this observation has no place today.

Gracious and loving heavenly Father, having seen how Your Church can live life, my prayer and deepest longing is this: give us another Pentecost. In Jesus' name we pray. Amen.

Order form

4 Easy Ways To Order

1. Phone in your credit card order: **01252 784700** (Mon–Fri, 9.30am – 4.30pm)
2. Visit our online store at **cwr.org.uk/shop**
3. Send this form together with your payment to: **CWR, Waverley Abbey House, Waverley Lane, Farnham, Surrey GU9 8EP**
4. Visit a Christian bookshop

For a list of our National Distributors, who supply countries outside the UK, visit cwr.org.uk/distributors

Your Details (required for orders and donations)

Full Name: CWR ID No. (if known):

Home Address:

Postcode:

Telephone No. (for queries):   Email:

Publications

TITLE	QTY	PRICE	TOTAL
Total Publications			

UK P&P: up to £24.99 = **£2.99**; £25.00 and over = **FREE**

Elsewhere P&P: up to £10 = **£4.95**; £10.01 – £50 = **£6.95**; £50.01 – £99.99 = **£10**; £100 and over = **£30**

Total Publications and P&P (please allow 14 days for delivery)   **A**

Subscriptions* (non direct debit)

	QTY	PRICE (including P&P)			TOTAL
		UK	Europe	Elsewhere	
Every Day with Jesus (1yr, 6 issues)		£16.95	£20.95	Please contact nearest National Distributor or CWR direct	
Large Print *Every Day with Jesus* (1yr, 6 issues)		£16.95	£20.95		
Inspiring Women Every Day (1yr, 6 issues)		£16.95	£20.95		
Life Every Day (Jeff Lucas) (1yr, 6 issues)		£16.95	£20.95		
Mettle: 15–18s (1yr, 3 issues)		£14.75	£17.60		
YP's: 11–14s (1yr, 6 issues)		£16.95	£20.95		
Topz: 7–11s (1yr, 6 issues)		£16.95	£20.95		

Total Subscriptions (subscription prices already include postage and packing)   **B**

Only use this section for subscriptions paid for by credit/debit card or cheque. For Direct Debit subscriptions see overleaf.

All CWR adult Bible reading notes are also available in **eBook** and **email subscription** format. Visit **cwr.org.uk** for further information.

Please circle which issue you would like your subscription to commence from:

JAN/FEB MAR/APR MAY/JUN JUL/AUG SEP/OCT NOV/DEC   Mettle JAN–APR MAY–AUG SEP–DEC

How would you like to hear from us?

We would love to keep you up to date on all aspects of the CWR ministry, including;
new publications, events & courses as well as how you can support us.

If you **DO** want to hear from us on email, please tick here [ ]

If you **DO NOT** want us to contact you by post, please tick here [ ]

Continued overleaf >>

You can update your preferences at any time by contacting our customer services team on 01252 784 700.
You can view our privacy policy online at cwr.org.uk

Payment Details

☐ I enclose a cheque/PO made payable to CWR for the amount of: £ _____

☐ Please charge my credit/debit card.

Cardholder's Name (in BLOCK CAPITALS) _____

Card No. ☐☐☐☐ ☐☐☐☐ ☐☐☐☐ ☐☐☐☐

Expires End ☐☐ ☐☐   Security Code ☐☐☐

Gift to CWR ☐ Please send me an acknowledgement of my gift   C ☐

Gift Aid (your home address required, see overleaf)

giftaid it I am a UK taxpayer and want CWR to reclaim the tax on all my donations for the four years prior to this ye**and on** all donations I make from the date of this Gift Aid declaration until further notice.*

Taxpayer's Full Name (in BLOCK CAPITALS) _____

Signature _____ **Date** _____

*I am a UK taxpayer and understand that if I pay less Income Tax and/or Capital Gains Tax than the amount of Gift Aid claimed on all my donations in that year it is my responsibility to pay any difference.

GRAND TOTAL (Total of A, B & C) ☐

Subscriptions by Direct Debit (UK bank account holders only)

One-year subscriptions cost £16.95 (except *Mettle*: £14.75) and include UK delivery. Please tick relevant boxes and fill in the form below.

☐ *Every Day with Jesus* (1yr, 6 issues)
☐ Large Print *Every Day with Jesus* (1yr, 6 issues)
☐ *Inspiring Women Every Day* (1yr, 6 issues)
☐ *Life Every Day* (Jeff Lucas) (1yr, 6 issues)

☐ *Mettle*: 15–18s (1yr, 3 issues)
☐ *YP's*: 11–14s (1yr, 6 issues)
☐ *Topz*: 7–11s (1yr, 6 issues)

Issue to commence from
☐ Jan/Feb ☐ Jul/Aug   *Mettle* ☐ Jan–Apr
☐ Mar/Apr ☐ Sep/Oct   ☐ May–Aug
☐ May/Jun ☐ Nov/Dec   ☐ Sep–Dec

CWR Instruction to your Bank or Building Society to pay by Direct Debit

DIRECT Debit

Please fill in the form and send to: CWR, Waverley Abbey House, Waverley Lane, Farnham, Surrey GU9 8EP

Name and full postal address of your Bank or Building Society

To: The Manager _____ Bank/Building Society

Address _____

Postcode _____

Name(s) of Account Holder(s)

Branch Sort Code ☐☐ ☐☐ ☐☐

Bank/Building Society Account Number ☐☐☐☐☐☐☐☐

Originator's Identification Number

4	2	0	4	8	7

Reference

Instruction to your Bank or Building Society

Please pay CWR Direct Debits from the account detailed in this Instruction subject to the safeguards assured by the Direct Debit Guarantee. I understand that this Instruction may remain with CWR and, if so, de will be passed electronically to my Bank/Building Society.

Signature(s) _____

Date _____

Banks and Building Societies may not accept Direct Debit Instructions for some types of account